JACQUELINE KENNEDY: THE WHITE HOUSE YEARS

Selections from the John F. Kennedy Library and Museum

JACQUELINE KENNEDY: THE WHITE HOUSE YEARS

Selections from the John F. Kennedy Library and Museum

Hamish Bowles

Arthur M. Schlesinger Jr.
Rachel Lambert Mellon

The Metropolitan Museum of Art, New York

A Bulfinch Press Book / Little, Brown and Company
Boston · New York · London

This publication is issued in conjunction with the exhibition
"Jacqueline Kennedy: The White House Years—Selections from the John F. Kennedy Library and Museum,"
held at The Metropolitan Museum of Art, New York, from May 1 through July 29, 2001.

The exhibition is made possible by L'ORÉAL.

Additional support has been provided by CONDÉ NAST.

The exhibition was organized by The Metropolitan Museum of Art, New York,
and the John F. Kennedy Library and Museum.

Published by The Metropolitan Museum of Art, New York, and Bulfinch Press.

Bulfinch Press is an imprint and trademark of Little, Brown and Company (Inc.).

First Edition, 2001

New color photography of clothing and accessories by Karin L. Willis of the Photograph Studio,
The Metropolitan Museum of Art

Additional photograph credits and copyrights appear on page 198.

Produced by The Metropolitan Museum of Art, New York
John P. O'Neill, Editor in Chief
Joan Holt and Jennifer Bernstein, Editors
Peter Antony, Production Manager

Sam Shahid and Company, Design
Charles D. Scheips Jr. and Stephanie Ovide Guarneri, Photograph Research

Separations by Professional Graphics, Rockford, Illinois
Printed and bound by Printer Industria Gráfica, S.A., Barcelona
Printing and binding coordinated by Ediciones El Viso, S.A., Madrid

Jacket/Cover Illustrations
Front: Photograph of Jacqueline Kennedy by Richard Avedon, January 3, 1961; ©1961 by Richard Avedon
Back: Evening gown by Oleg Cassini, worn at the inaugural gala, January 19, 1961; photograph by Karin L. Willis

Frontispiece
Photograph of Jacqueline Kennedy by Mark Shaw/Photo Researchers

Library of Congress Cataloging-in-Publication Data

Jacqueline Kennedy: the White House Years / selections from the John F. Kennedy Library and Museum / [compiled and edited by] Hamish Bowles; with essays by Arthur M. Schlesinger, Jr., Rachel Lambert Mellon, and Hamish Bowles.
p. cm.
Catalog to accompany exhibition at the Metropolitan Museum of Art, May–July 2001,
and at the John F. Kennedy Library and Museum in fall 2001.
ISBN 0-87099-981-8 (alk. paper)—ISBN 0-87099-982-6 (pbl.: alk. paper)—ISBN 0-8212-2745-9 (Bulfinch Press)
1. Onassis, Jacqueline Kennedy, 1929–1994—Exhibitions.
2. Onassis, Jacqueline Kennedy, 1929–1994—Influence Exhibitions.
3. Onassis, Jacqueline Kennedy, 1929–1994—Clothing—Exhibitions.
4. Presidents' spouses—United States—Biography—Exhibitions.
I. Bowles, Hamish II. Metropolitan Museum of Art (New York, N.Y.) III. John F. Kennedy Library and Museum

E843.O53 J33 2001
973.922'092—dc21 00-066237

Contents

Director's Foreword vi
The Metropolitan Museum of Art

President's Foreword vii
John F. Kennedy Library Foundation

Sponsor's Statement ix

Jacqueline Kennedy in the White House 3
Arthur M. Schlesinger Jr.

Jacqueline Bouvier Kennedy: A Reminiscence 13
Rachel Lambert Mellon

Defining Style: Jacqueline Kennedy's White House Years 17
Hamish Bowles

Campaign 37

Inauguration 55

White House Style 69

Travel 115

Hats 179

Riding 185

Jacqueline Bouvier Kennedy: A Time Line, 1929–1994 188

Notes on Sources 194

Bibliography 195

Acknowledgments 196

Photograph Credits 198

In 1960, at age thirty-one, Jacqueline Bouvier Kennedy was the youngest wife ever of an American president-elect. It is all the more amazing, given her youth, that she so profoundly influenced American taste during her years in the White House. She brought style and grace to her duties as first lady and provided a striking visual image that reflected the promise of her husband's administration. Although she attempted to temper the level of public interest in her appearance, fascination with her style never abated. We are pleased, therefore, to share the timeless impact of her fashion legacy in the exhibition "Jacqueline Kennedy: The White House Years—Selections from the John F. Kennedy Library and Museum."

The clothing and accessories presented in the exhibition were given to the Kennedy Library by Mrs. Kennedy because she understood the importance of dress to the complete representation of a specific moment in time. Her well-established belief in the historical resonance of art and architecture led her, not surprisingly, to consider it appropriate that key elements of her formal White House wardrobe be placed in the Library's archives.

The Metropolitan Museum's partnership with the John F. Kennedy Library and Museum has resulted in a fruitful sharing of methodologies and interpretations of the clothing donated by Mrs. Kennedy to that institution. The Costume Institute's primary mandate is to collect and display apparel of aesthetic significance. In the former first lady's wardrobe the originality and workmanship of some of the best designers of the day can be seen, along with the more particular manifestations of the sensibilities of the client, who heeded not only her own preferences but also the needs of protocol and of the media. Thus, in our galleries, these garments held by the Kennedy Library, and valued in that context for their historical associations, have the expanded implications of an aesthetic response to the highly public and ceremonial role of first lady.

Jacqueline Kennedy's association with the Museum was long-standing. As wife of the president she personally chose the Temple of Dendur as Egypt's gift to the American people in recognition of the contribution of the United States toward saving the temples at Abu Simbel. Now housed here at the Metropolitan alongside our great collection of Egyptian art, it reminds us of her importance to our institutional life. As an editor at Viking Press, she worked with our former special consultant, Diana Vreeland, on books associated with the Costume Institute. And, as is perhaps less widely known, Mrs. Kennedy donated a number of dresses to our costume collection.

The exhibition and this publication are the work of Hamish Bowles, European editor at large of *Vogue* and our consultant for this project, who has written numerous articles on design and costume history. Two additional contributors to this volume are Arthur M. Schlesinger Jr., former special assistant to President Kennedy and author of *A Thousand Days: John F. Kennedy in the White House,* which won the Pulitzer Prize for biography in 1966; and Rachel Lambert Mellon, designer of the White House Rose Garden during the Kennedy administration.

The Metropolitan Museum is extremely grateful to L'Oréal for its outstanding support of the exhibition. We are also indebted to Condé Nast for its important contribution toward the realization of the project.

Philippe de Montebello
Director, The Metropolitan Museum of Art

On behalf of my family and the John F. Kennedy Library and Museum, I want to welcome visitors to the exhibition "Jacqueline Kennedy: The White House Years—Selections from the John F. Kennedy Library and Museum."

My parents shared a deep knowledge and love of history. While my father's interests tended toward the parliamentary and political, my mother was drawn to the personal and poetic. She used to say with bemused admiration that my father had finished Winston Churchill's life of Marlborough on the way to the airport, yet she always claimed to have learned most about what to expect from life in the White House by reading the eighteenth-century memoirs of the duc de Saint-Simon on the campaign trail in 1960.

My mother was able to evoke the lives and people of other times and places, describing the personalities of the ancient pharaohs, the intrigues of European court society, or life on a Nantucket whaling ship so vividly that, as children, John and I felt we had visited these wondrous places.

So it was no surprise to those who knew Jacqueline Kennedy that it was her passion for history that guided and informed her work in the White House. She wanted to share her knowledge and excitement about the past with all Americans, especially children. She recognized that to a child, American history is often a rather dry and dull affair, and she saw a visit to the president's house as a chance to spark each child's interest in the people who made our country what it has become. In addition, she was a patriot. Like President Kennedy, she believed that American civilization had come of age. Together, they transformed the White House into an international stage celebrating American arts and letters and encouraged Americans to take pride in our artistic as well as our political heritage.

My mother regarded her time in the White House as an extraordinary gift. She knew she had been given the chance to play a part in history and worked hard to be worthy of the honor. When that period of her life came to an end, she worked just as hard to ensure that the history of that time would be preserved and made available to future generations.

Today, the John F. Kennedy Library and Museum carries on that work. Together with my aunts and uncles, my mother dedicated the Library to "all those who, through the art of politics, seek a new and better world." Even as people are captivated by Jacqueline Kennedy's style and grace, I hope that this exhibition will give visitors a greater understanding of the part she played in that quest and how much there is yet to do.

Caroline Kennedy
President, John F. Kennedy Library Foundation

L'Oréal is proud to be sponsoring "Jacqueline Kennedy: The White House Years—Selections from the John F. Kennedy Library and Museum," an exhibition organized by The Metropolitan Museum of Art, New York, and the John F. Kennedy Library and Museum, Boston. The exhibition, which marks the fortieth anniversary of Jacqueline Kennedy's emergence as America's first lady, is an opportunity to celebrate a woman who brought elegance, intelligence, and cultivated taste to all that she did. Her passion for the arts, her beauty, and her style have had a lasting impact on America's cultural heritage.

Featured in the exhibition are more than eighty original costumes, including many of the pieces Mrs. Kennedy wore during her historic visit to Paris in 1961 with her husband, President Kennedy. The cordial and warm relationship she developed with Charles de Gaulle, then president of France, is part of the lore of that time and is often credited with helping to renew French-American relations.

On behalf of L'Oréal, I hope that you delight in this exhibition and gain from it new insight into the life of a woman who remains an icon of style and culture.

Guy Peyrelongue
President and CEO, L'Oréal USA

The White House, watercolor painted by Jacqueline Kennedy about 1961. In the picture are (at the top) Pierre Salinger with members of the press, the Kennedys with Caroline, John's carriage on the balcony, nanny Maud Shaw (in yellow), and Letitia Baldrige (lower right) with a group of bagpipers.

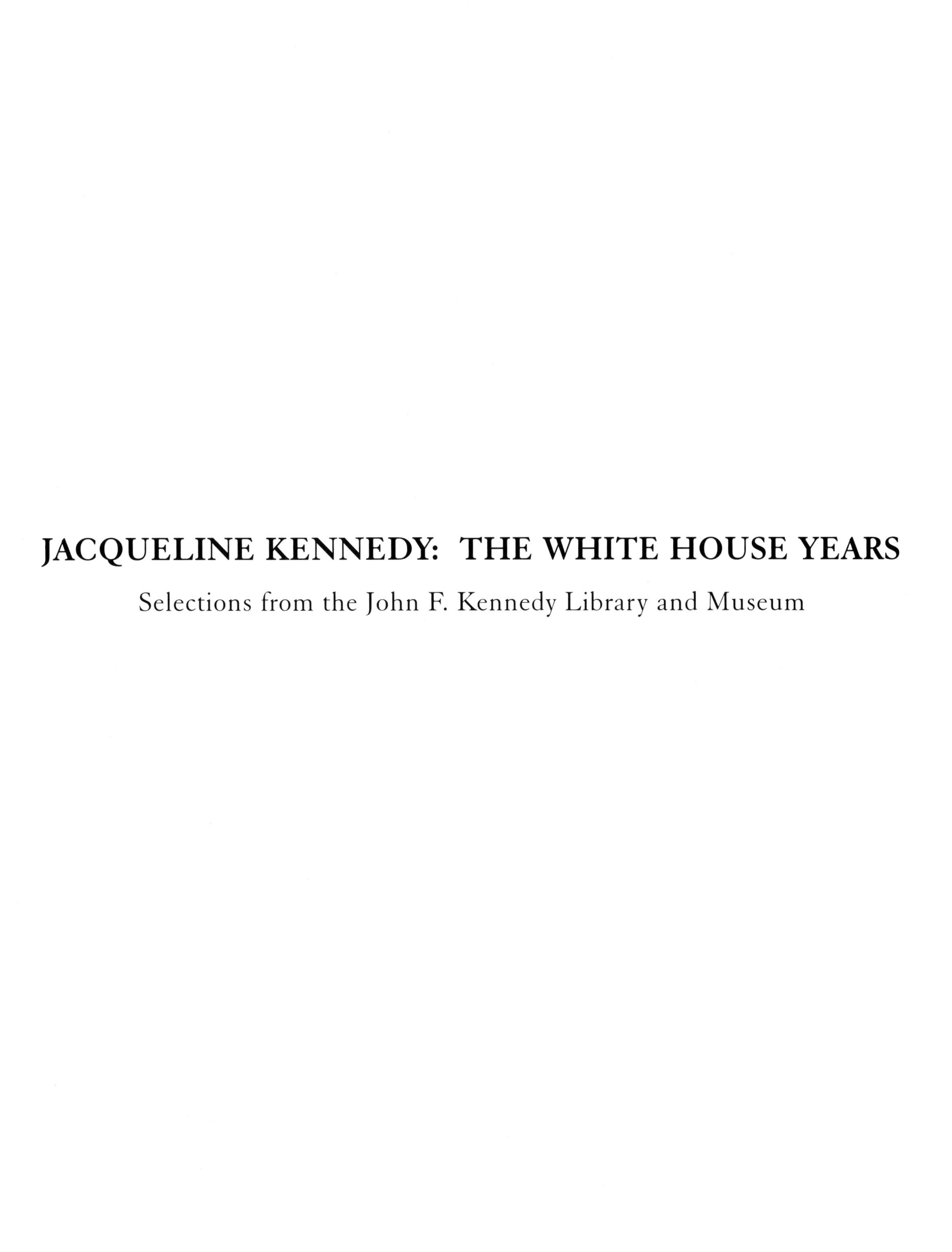

JACQUELINE KENNEDY: THE WHITE HOUSE YEARS

Selections from the John F. Kennedy Library and Museum

Jacqueline Kennedy in the White House

Arthur M. Schlesinger Jr.

Being the first lady, Hillary Rodham Clinton has said, isn't a job—"it's a role."

Jacqueline Bouvier Kennedy was thirty-one years old at the inauguration of the thirty-fifth president, John Fitzgerald Kennedy. She was by nine years the youngest presidential wife to enter the White House with her husband. (Tyler and Cleveland married still younger women but did so in the White House.) Like thirty presidential wives before her (Jefferson, Jackson, Van Buren, and Arthur were widowers; Buchanan was a bachelor), Jacqueline Kennedy confronted the challenge of figuring out a role as first lady.

She hated the title and instructed the staff that she should be known, not as first lady, but as Mrs. Kennedy. Carl Sferrazza Anthony, the historian of first ladies, traces the title to President Zachary Taylor's eulogy at Dolley Madison's funeral in 1849. Mrs. Kennedy thought the term undemocratic; also, "First Lady" sounded to her like the name of a saddle horse. Eventually, she acquiesced in the usage.

She was a young woman of notable beauty, at once wistful and luminous, and of acute intelligence and exacting expectation. She had been reared in a class, a time—the 1940s—and a place—Newport, Rhode Island—where young ladies were taught to conceal their brains lest they frighten young men away. She observed upper-class conventions, but underneath a veil of lovely inconsequence she developed a cool assessment of people and an ironical slant on life. One soon realized that her social graces masked tremendous awareness, an all-seeing eye, ruthless judgment, and a steely purpose.

Jacqueline Kennedy brought several unusual qualities with her to the White House. One was a knowledge of the arts. Her response to life was aesthetic rather than intellectual or moralistic. When she won *Vogue*'s Prix de Paris in 1951, she wrote that the three men she would most like to have known were Baudelaire, Wilde, and Diaghilev. Her natural habitat was the international world of society and art. Bernard Berenson once cautioned her that "American girls should marry American boys. They wear better."

Her husband, an American boy, was wholly sympathetic to his wife's artistic leanings, though his own tastes ran to literature and architecture more than to music and decor. He asked Robert Frost to read a poem at his inauguration and embraced a proposal by Kay Halle, a Kennedy friend, that leading writers and artists be invited to the ceremony. This idea rather annoyed the politicians on the Inauguration Committee who were hoarding tickets, but it went through, and W. H. Auden, Robert Lowell, Alexis Léger, Jacques Maritain, John Steinbeck, John Hersey, Allen Tate, and fifty other writers, composers, and painters were in the audience. "What a joy," said Steinbeck, "that literacy is no longer prima facie evidence of treason." "Thank you," said Lincoln Kirstein, "for restoring to the United States the pleasures and powers of the mind."

To her appreciation of the arts Jacqueline Kennedy added a passionate sense of history. She liked to know how things began and how they evolved, and her glamorous modernity was based on an intense curiosity about the past. "We would tour the battlegrounds," Edward M. Kennedy recalled of the 1950s, "and my brother and Jackie knew everything about the Civil War." "She had a fantastic desire for historical knowledge," said Letitia Baldrige, her social secretary, "and she was a sponge once she learned it."

And she knew Washington. She had lived there for eighteen years, had been a photographer and columnist for the Washington *Times-Herald*, and had absorbed the distinctive atmosphere of what Henry James called the City of Conversation. Her *Times-Herald* columns show a particular interest in the White House and its occupants. Though she had the reputation of being indifferent or even hostile to political life, she came in fact to enjoy politicians and their free and easy talk. As a senator's wife, she often attended debates and hearings, and in due course she also came rather to like campaigning.

Jacqueline Kennedy had thought hard about her new role as the president's wife. With her historical sense, she understood that the White House was not a private residence but the property of the American people. She also hoped to use the White

Opposite: Jacqueline Kennedy and Senator John F. Kennedy, photographed by Mark Shaw in Hyannis Port, Cape Cod, Massachusetts, 1959

House to honor achievement in the arts. Before the inauguration, Letitia Baldrige announced to the press, "Mrs. Kennedy plans to make the White House a showcase for great American art and artists."

During the interregnum between the election and the inauguration, she carefully studied books and files on the executive mansion supplied to her by the Library of Congress. Mrs. Eisenhower gave her a tour of the White House. "As soon as she left," said Jacqueline Kennedy's friend Mrs. Henry (Sister) Parish, the famed interior decorator, "she called me, and it was then that I realized that Jackie did not have two big eyes—she had dozens. Every room was observed, down to the last detail." The day after the visit Mrs. Eisenhower told J. B. West, the White House chief usher—in the voice, he noted, that she reserved for disapproval—"She's planning to redo every room in this house. You've got *quite* a project ahead of you."

In a phrase much used in the City of Conversation, Jacqueline Kennedy hit the ground running. On her first working day as the president's wife she discussed with David Finley, the chairman of the federal Commission of Fine Arts, ways and means of soliciting gifts that would reclaim for the White House its historic integrity—perhaps a committee to raise funds for that purpose? Finley was so delighted that he made the first gift himself: a splendid eighteenth-century walnut highboy in the Chippendale style.

Sister Parish arrived at the White House two days after the inauguration. (Her nickname caused some confusion. One newspaper ran the headline KENNEDYS PICK NUN TO DECORATE WHITE HOUSE.) Her inspection was unsparing. The rooms used for state functions on the first floor were, she thought, "tattered, worn, and seemed to have no rhyme or reason. I felt sad for the neglected rooms. It disturbed me to know that these badly designed, poorly maintained rooms belonged to the United States. . . . What did the kings and queens and great statesmen of the world think when they came to our president's home?" As for the family room on the second floor, "the Eisenhowers had given it a cold, stiff hotel look, and it was all there, including the TV sets."

Three days after the inauguration Mrs. Kennedy had George Balanchine for tea (the great choreographer wondered whether the White House might provide anything stronger). She asked him, "What can I do for the arts?" Like Finley, Balanchine was delighted by her and afterward observed to a reporter, "She looked like a pussy-cat." Later he told her that she should become the "spiritual savior" of America. "I don't mean in a religious sense," he wrote, "but I mean to distinguish between material things and things of the spirit—art, beauty. No one else can take care of these things. You alone can—if you will."

Mrs. Kennedy had more limited objectives. Her first priority was to become spiritual savior of the White House. Even here she proceeded with caution, afraid that she might seem officious in calling for changes. Her husband reinforced her apprehensions. Americans, the new president feared, did not like presidents or their wives fooling around with the White House. President Truman, when he dared to build a second-floor balcony on the south portico, provoked such wrath that he felt he was being accused of interfering with the natural order of the universe. How to rehabilitate the White House without rousing a political storm?

President Kennedy now turned to Clark Clifford, not only a trusted adviser and personal attorney but a veteran of the Truman wars. At luncheon with the Kennedys two weeks after the inauguration, Clifford recalled the outcry against the balcony. President Truman, he added, had wanted to match the historic tradition of the White House with furnishings equally historic, but funds had not been available and the result, Clifford said, was the "somewhat pathetic and shabby air the building had acquired during the Eisenhower years."

Still, thousands of visitors came through the White House every day, Jacqueline Kennedy reminded the group at lunch, "We must make this building something that they will be proud of. I want to make the White House the first house in the land." And she also envisaged the White House as a history lesson. "People who visit the White House see practically nothing that dates before 1902. People should see things that develop their sense of history."

Clifford endorsed the objective but warned that great care had to be taken. "The White House is a sacred cow to the American people and woe to any president who touches it without preparing the groundwork." A fine arts committee for the White House, he suggested, might provide legal and political cover. President Kennedy seized upon the idea; Clifford drew up the legal framework; and on February 23, 1961, hardly a month after the inauguration, the Fine Arts Committee for the White House came into existence as a body empowered to "locate authentic furniture of the date of the building of the White House [1802] and the raising of funds to purchase this furniture as gifts for the White House."

The original formulation seemed to restrict the restoration to *objets* of the very early republic. *Life* ran a jocose editorial entitled "Forward to 1802." Mrs. Kennedy soon clarified her purpose. "The White House," she said in an interview, "does and must continue to represent the living, evolving character of the Executive Branch of the National Government. Its occupants have been persons of widely different geographical, social and economic backgrounds, and accordingly of different cultural and intellectual tastes—it would therefore be highly inadvisable, even if it were possible, to fix on a single style of decorating and furnishings for a building that ought to reflect the whole history of the Presidency."

"This," she continued, "should put to rest the fears of people who think we might restore the building to its earliest period, leaving [out] all that came after; or fill it with French furniture; or hang modern pictures all over it—and paint it whatever color we like. The White House belongs to our past and no one who cares about our past would treat it that way."

The Kennedys' friend Charles Wrightsman, whose wife Jayne played a generous and resourceful role in the restoration, proposed as chairman of the new committee Henry Francis du Pont, the founder of the Winterthur Museum in Delaware, a noted authority on and collector of American antiques, a millionaire, and also a Republican. Though eighty-one years old, du Pont accepted the assignment. It was, Jacqueline Kennedy said, "the biggest red-letter day of all. . . . Without him on the Committee I didn't think we would accomplish much—and with him I knew there would be no criticism."

The fourteen members of the committee—eight women, six men—gave generous support in funds as well as in artifacts, and the restoration was rapidly under way. None of this would have worked, however, without the wholehearted collaboration of the chief usher, who, despite his title, was not an usher at all but the general manager of the White House.

Mrs. Eisenhower's prediction was right: the chief usher had *quite* a project ahead of him. But J. B. West, who had started out at the White House in the Roosevelt years and had been chief usher since 1957, applauded the restoration. "Mr. West," said Sister Parish, "was a fund of knowledge and unceasingly helpful. Nothing was too much in his desire to help us." "He was ever patient and understanding," said Letitia Baldrige. "He went through a terrible lot. He had to referee everybody's fight and never say no to the Kennedys."

And he delighted in Mrs. Kennedy. His memoir, *Upstairs in the White House* (1973), offers a vivid description of her modus operandi. "I soon learned that Mrs. Kennedy's wish, murmured with a 'Do you think . . .' or 'Could you please . . . ,' was as much a command as Mrs. Eisenhower's 'I want this done immediately.'" The new first lady, West said, turned the White House inside out and imprinted her own style upon the mansion. "In public, she was elegant, aloof, dignified, and regal. In private, she was casual, impish, and irreverent. She had a will of iron, with more determination than anyone I have ever met. Yet she was so soft-spoken, so deft and subtle, that she could impose that will upon people without their ever knowing it."

Relaxed and uninhibited, she was always popping up everywhere, wearing slacks, kicking off her shoes, sitting on the floor, hair flying in every direction. She poked fun at everything, including herself. She was highly organized but rarely held herself to a schedule. She conducted "spelunking" expeditions into dusty storerooms and warehouses in search of forgotten treasures. She had, West observed, a "total mastery of detail—endless, endless detail." West found himself "thoroughly enjoying the most creative and challenging work to which the Chief Usher had ever been put."

Jacqueline Kennedy's chosen medium of communication was a memorandum on a legal pad, scrawled upon in the looping society handwriting she had learned at Miss Porter's. She fired memos off every morning, rather in the manner of the "Action This Day" memos with which Winston Churchill used to torment generals, admirals, and cabinet ministers during the Second World War.

In conjunction with the work of the Fine Arts Committee for the White House, the Paintings Committee was formed by Mrs. Kennedy. Shown with her in the Green Room in December 1961 are the committee's chairman, James Fosburgh (on the couch), and, standing behind him, Henry du Pont, chairman of the Fine Arts Committee.

Showing impressive executive ability, Jacqueline Kennedy skillfully managed an unruly team. Du Pont was to be the authority on historic furnishings, but, recalling that President Monroe had furnished the White House in the French Empire style, the first lady chose Stéphane Boudin of the Jansen firm in Paris as the authority on decoration. "From the first day the two men met," J. B. West noted, "it was apparent they'd never see eye to eye on anything. Mr. du Pont, a dignified Eastern millionaire, was interested only in authenticity, and didn't care about arrangement or proportion or compatibility. M. Boudin, a bubbly, dramatic little Frenchman, cared only about pleasing the eye."

Jacqueline Kennedy, confident of her own taste and charm, kept them working together. "Next time Mr. du P comes," one of her memos to West reads, "the poor man can't bear to think our moving days are over—he enjoyed it so—tell him Mrs. K loves the rooms the way they are and doesn't want to make any more changes—the press and Maxine Cheshire [of the Washington *Post*] . . . write rather nasty stories and Mrs. K feels it may undermine work of committee etc. etc. I am sorry he wastes your time but I don't dare tell him. . . . Put him off until we have LOTS of new furniture—or he can come on his way back from Fla to see 3rd floor & Q[ueens] room (and not change ANYTHING)."

She quietly favored Boudin. A memo: "Mr. West. Could you send Mr. du Pont Boudin's 3 samples for green room 1) big ocean on green design 2) smaller green-on-green piece 3) tiny bit more of moiré. Also return him his own darker green stripe material—on white board. Please enclose this humble letter soliciting his approval—If we don't get it he will have the shock of me doing it anyway."

There was tension, too, between Boudin and Sister Parish. This did not work out so affably. A coolness arose between Mrs. Parish and Mrs. Kennedy. "Finally, I learned the source of our problem," Mrs. Parish later said. "She had been told that I had kicked Caroline, and she was convinced it was true." Sister's granddaughter commented, "I wouldn't have put it past her, but that was not the root of the falling-out," and attributed it instead to a dispute over money. Indeed, Mrs. Kennedy felt that she had been overcharged for modest work in Glen Ora, the Kennedys' country house. In any case, Mrs. Parish's specialty was creating small, cozy rooms. Boudin was better able to cope with the state rooms of the White House.

Jacqueline Kennedy was a mistress of meticulous detail. On the Treaty Room, which had served as the Cabinet Room before Theodore Roosevelt built the West Wing: "Mr. West. I was looking at treaties—in Treaty Room. a) They should all be ones that were signed in that room. That would be [Andrew] Johnson—TR—isn't that right? Or did J Q Adams use that as office and sign treaties there—? Is there any way of finding out which were signed in office—when room was that—and which when it was Cabinet Room—probably not. So I think—as Treaty of Peace with Spain is obviously in that room—we should just have Johnson—TR—and lots more. Let's get rid of FDR and Cuba—and get lots more treaties of 1864–1902. We could put them way up [on] walls. b) Where the name of treaty is printed on the mat—I think date should be printed also—as it is too complicated to read treaty to find out."

The Queens' Bedroom for distinguished guests, like Winston Churchill and V. M. Molotov, was the subject of a number of Jacqueline Kennedy's bullets: "Mr. West. When was mantel put in Queens room—1902; 1948? I don't really want to change it. If it's 1948 will you send photo to Boudin and ask him if he thinks we should get lower, more English one." It all came out well: "Mr. West. The Queens' room is INCREDIBLE. It really could be [fit] for a Queen now."

Before their falling out, Sister Parish had arranged for Amory Houghton of Corning Glass to make Steuben wineglasses engraved with the Great Seal of the United States. Mrs. Kennedy's refusal displays her social consciousness as well as her skill in maneuver. She had already purchased wineglasses she loved from West Virginia and, as she explained to Mrs. Parish, at "one millionth the price." Nor did she miss the Great Seal. "It is almost a relief. Our flatware and china are all engraved."

Then she added: "West Virginia is the most unemployed area in the country and . . . I just don't want to put a lot of people in West Virginia out of work now, especially as so many of them found jobs because of this glass." She was sure, she continued, that Mr. Houghton would understand her concern. "The thing I would really love to have from him is the marvelous English furniture for the Queens' Room, so you might try that tack. Do be sure to let him know that you had not consulted me when you thought of this."

President Kennedy no doubt was all in favor of protecting the West Virginia glass workers and, when his own domain was involved, had no hesitation about registering preferences. "Mr. West—JFK approves Cabinet Room curtains—does not like muddy colors of rug. . . . His office. We don't want white chairs—he wants to see sample of rug. He says curtains are OK—but I think perhaps they should be a creamier color—as it makes everything else in room look so dirty & we can't make sofas white—what does B[oudin] suggest for sofa? I just think design might be a bit feminine for Pres office—I like something less draped—more like Cabinet or Red Room curtains."

When she traveled, she would dictate instructions through the U. S. Signal Corps. Once she recommended from abroad that historical items be put in glass-paneled cases, or "tastefully designed vitrines." This was unluckily transcribed and distributed as "tastefully designed latrines," resulting in much high-level merriment.

The Fine Arts Committee for the White House and its devoted members sent out pleas for furniture, paintings, busts, chandeliers, and rugs that had been or might have been at one time or another in the executive mansion. They were astonished by the response. "The White House," said J. B. West, "was barraged with everybody's old quilts, spittoons, and paintings." Many items were hopeless; some were genuine finds.

Meanwhile, Jacqueline Kennedy had focused on a new White House need—a permanent collection of American paintings. Most paintings on White House walls were portraits of presidents and their wives. In many cases these were poor copies of vanished originals. A Special Committee for White House Paintings was set up, headed by the artist James W. Fosburgh. Within two years the committee gathered for the White House more than one hundred and fifty paintings, drawings, prints, and sculptures.

Other items were offered for purchase. "Mr. West. I so like the rug, but we are short of dollars and I am ENRAGED at everyone trying to gyp the White House. Tell him if he gives it he can get a tax deduction and photo in our book—if not—goodbye!" The costs of the restoration project far exceeded the White House allocation in the federal budget. "They don't even have a brochure for all the tourists who go through here," Mrs. Kennedy told the chief usher. "But if we could *sell* one, we could finance the restoration."

President Kennedy hesitated at first, fearing criticism over the commercialization of the president's house. Once again Clark Clifford came to the rescue, proposing the creation of a nonprofit organization. On November 3, 1961, the White House Historical Association came into existence. Its first assignment was to produce a White House guidebook, an undertaking in which Mrs. Kennedy took an intense personal interest.

"This must be scholarly—and not talk down to the public—then they will learn from it—and I have never seen a case, in politics or books, when talking down did any good—it just bores people. . . . This shall be something which Berenson, Uncle Lefty and Arthur Schlesinger would want to read." (Uncle Lefty was Wilmarth Lewis, the Horace Walpole scholar and Jacqueline Kennedy's stepfather's brother-in-law.)

The author of *The White House: An Historic Guide* was Lorraine Pearce, the first occupant of the Jacqueline Kennedy–created position of White House curator. Mrs. Kennedy herself submitted the text to rigorous editing. The National Geographic Society provided the illustrations and supervised the publication. The guidebook proved to be a smash. More than six hundred thousand copies were sold in the Kennedy years, and it has been selling steadily ever since. Having helped pay for the Kennedy restoration, the White House Historical Association devoted the guidebook proceeds to additional historical furnishings and paintings.

By this time Jacqueline Kennedy's restoration project, despite initial doubts, had won enthusiastic national support—confirmed by the popular success in February 1962 of the CBS program "A Tour of the White House with Mrs. John F. Kennedy." It was, Theodore H. White said, "the most successful nonfiction show" CBS had ever presented. (Norman Mailer filed a dissent in an article for *Esquire*: "I liked her, I like her still, but she was a

The front cover of *The White House: An Historic Guide*, the first edition of which was published in June 1962 by the White House Historical Association

phony—it was the cruelest thing one could say, she was a royal phony." Jacqueline Kennedy later confided that she rather agreed with Mailer's account of the image she presented on television.)

The guidebook's success led her to her next project and the White House Historical Association's next production—a guide to the presidents. She wanted, she wrote me, something so "someone like me can get a vague but interesting idea of each Pres (for instance I haven't a clue what party Pierce or Buchanan were of or what they did—except fail)." There should be a "lively, even controversial, big sketch (not just born, married, wrote Monroe Doctrine, died) with some description of their character. . . . It must be short enough so people will read it all—in other words all on one page. . . . I would hope they wouldn't have more (except in some cases you'll have to) as that detracts from the concision I want. So many people and children are lazy—if they can learn something in a glance at a page—they will do it—rather than thumb through a history book."

"If you can do all this," she said, "I will carve your name on the Blue Room mantelpiece. It's your penance for not coming to India when we were there." Then she sketched herself in a nightgown with arms outstretched, walking down a corridor past busts marked Lincoln and Washington. She and I had seen together Alain Resnais's haunting film *Last Year in Marienbad*, and her caption under the sketch read: "Last yr. in the White House I was looking for Arthur Schlesinger—where is he—behind what door—down the long corridors past the statues—is he writing the guidebook, or is it only a dream?"

It was, alas, only a dream. Despite this irresistible plea, I couldn't do the presidents myself. Her husband had other ideas about how I should spend my time. But I prevailed on my Harvard colleague Frank Freidel, the biographer of Franklin Roosevelt, to undertake the text, which he discharged with style and speed. The National Geographic Society again produced the book as a public service.

Her next idea was a working library for the White House. A small room on the ground floor contained a random assemblage of volumes, but the White House had no serious collection of fundamental works on American history. Here, again, I was enlisted as the first lady's point man. What we had in mind were the "American Classics"—the two thousand or so volumes most essential to an understanding of the American experience. James T. Babb Jr., the Yale University librarian, headed the selection committee. Jacqueline Kennedy directed the committee to choose the "writings that have influenced American thinking—Locke etc. and all books by Presidents . . . just what a gentleman's library should look like."

The restoration of the White House was the first step in a larger vision. "President Kennedy and I," she said in later years, "shared the conviction that the artist should be honored by society, and all of this had to do with calling attention to what was finest in America, what should be esteemed and honored. The arts had been treated as a stepchild in the United States. When the government had supported the arts, as in many WPA projects, artists were given a hand, and many wonderful things emerged. . . . Our great museums and great performing companies should of course be supported, but the experimental and the unknown should also be thrown a line. Our contemporary artists—in all the media—have excited the world. It was so sad that we couldn't help them more. Of course, the president and I talked of these things. It was something he responded to and cared about for his country. Who else had had a poet read at his inauguration, and so many great writers invited to it?"

The first lady had strong White House support beyond her own staff. Pierre Salinger, the president's press secretary, had started out as a concert pianist before turning to journalism, and he retained a lively interest in the arts. Richard Goodwin was a constant source of imaginative ideas about government encouragement of the arts. I, too, helped where I could.

An important unofficial adviser was William Walton, a journalist, painter, and confidant of both Kennedys (he had run the presidential campaign in New York in 1960), who eventually succeeded David Finley as chairman of the Commission of Fine Arts. The Kennedys were wholly unaffected in their attitude toward the arts, Walton explained; it was simply that they were "susceptible to the comfort of the arts. They couldn't live without them—it was woven into the pattern of their lives."

White House dinners afforded opportunities to recognize and celebrate the importance of the arts and of artists. In November 1961 Pablo Casals, who had long declined to play his cello in public until democracy was restored in Spain, agreed to perform at the White House on an evening honoring Governor Luis Muñoz Marín of Puerto Rico. Kennedy said with emphasis in introducing Casals: "We believe that an artist, in order to be true to himself and his work, must be a free man."

Other dinners followed: for Igor Stravinsky; for the western hemisphere's Nobel prizewinners (whom Kennedy famously called "the most extraordinary collection of talent, of human knowledge, that has ever been gathered together at the White House, with the possible exception of when Thomas Jefferson dined alone"); for André Malraux (at which Kennedy began his toast by saying, "This will be the first speech about relations between France and the United States that does not include a tribute to General Lafayette"). And dinners in honor of visiting statesmen or monarchs always included artists and writers and entertainment of high quality. The administration, Thornton Wilder said, had created "a whole new world of surprised self-respect" in the arts.

Jacqueline Kennedy played a dazzling role in the White House dinners. She enjoyed especially the one for Malraux. After John Kennedy met Malraux in Paris in 1961, I asked him what the adventurous author of *Man's Fate* was like. The president said wryly, "He was far more interested in Jackie than in me—which I perfectly understand." When Malraux came to Washington in May 1962, the Kennedys summoned an impressive list of American writers and artists to meet him: Edmund Wilson, Leonard Bernstein, Elia Kazan, Robert Lowell, Archibald MacLeish, Saul Bellow, Arthur Miller, Isaac Stern, Robert Penn Warren, Tennessee Williams. (Later, sitting next to Mme Malraux at a dinner at the French embassy, I asked her what American writers were admired in France. She named William Faulkner, of course, then paused for a minute and named Margaret Mitchell. When my reaction betrayed surprise, she said, "Oh, and my husband admires her too—he found Gone with the Wind fascinating.")

John F. Kennedy's reaction to most problems was "OK, but what can we do about it?" The national government, he noted, did all sorts of things within its own jurisdiction that bore upon the arts, from erecting public buildings to designing stamps. Here was an opportunity to set standards that might serve as examples to the rest of the country. In the summer of 1961 he asked Pierre Salinger and me to consider how the White House might take hold of this problem. We recommended that he appoint a special consultant on the arts to survey the areas where government policy had impact on cultural life and to define the elements of a national cultural program.

In December, after the success of the Casals dinner, the president invited August Heckscher of the Twentieth Century Fund to conduct "without fanfare" an inquiry into the resources, limitations, and potentialities of national policy in relation to the arts. "Obviously government can at best play only a marginal role in our cultural affairs," he told Heckscher. "But I would like to think that it is making its full contribution in this role."

Heckscher looked first at the question of whether government kept its own house in beauty and fitness. Government was, after all, "the great builder, the coiner, the printer, the purchaser of art, the commissioner of works of art, the guardian of great collections, the setter of standards for good or for bad in innumerable fields."

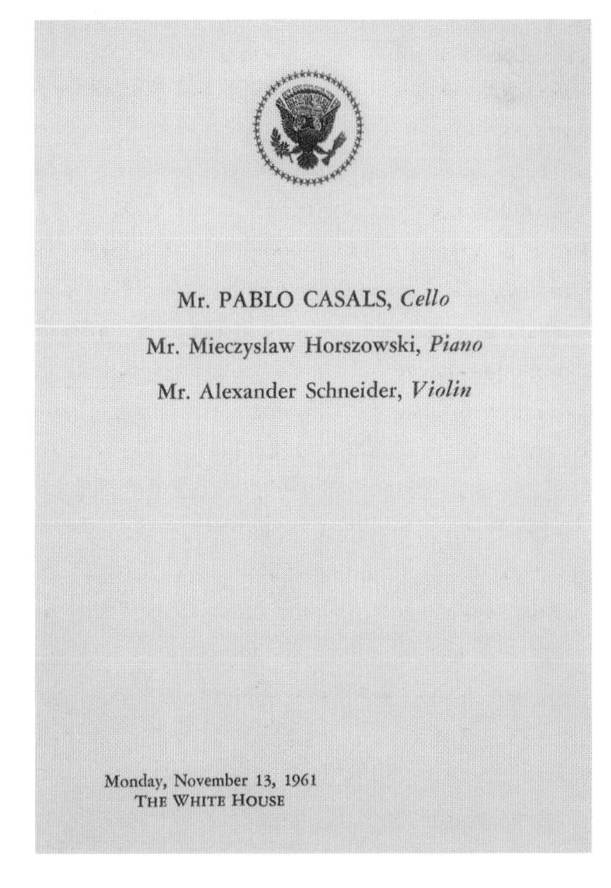
Mr. PABLO CASALS, *Cello*

Mr. Mieczyslaw Horszowski, *Piano*

Mr. Alexander Schneider, *Violin*

Monday, November 13, 1961
THE WHITE HOUSE

Opposite: A sketch by Jacqueline Kennedy, sent to the author at the time she asked him to write a guide to the presidents. This page: Casals played after the state dinner for Governor Muñoz Marín of Puerto Rico on November 13, 1961.

He reviewed the impact of tax and tariff laws on artists and artistic institutions. He proposed an advisory council on the arts and, as "the logical crowning step in a national cultural policy," a national arts foundation. In the spring of 1963 he put these and other recommendations in a report entitled "The Arts and the National Government."

A few days later, the president set up the Advisory Council on the Arts by executive order and prepared to make the Special Consultancy on the Arts a full-time and permanent office. The Heckscher report laid the basis for the National Endowments for the Arts and the Humanities soon to be established in the Johnson administration. Since Heckscher wished to return to the Twentieth Century Fund, Jacqueline Kennedy proposed Richard Goodwin as his successor. Goodwin hesitated (and the president said to me, "Why the hell does Dick want that job anyway?!"), but Mrs. Kennedy sent him a most beguiling and persuasive letter that closed the deal. Goodwin saw the special consultancy as a way of approaching the whole problem of the aesthetics of American society—the way our cities looked and the beauty of our environment, along with general encouragement of the arts.

Washington had always been a company town, dominated by government and politics, and Jacqueline Kennedy wanted to make it, like Paris and London, the cultural as well as the political capital. The Eisenhower administration had endorsed proposals for a national cultural center, and Mrs. Kennedy hoped for something along the lines of Lincoln Center in New York City. The project became in due course the John F. Kennedy Center for the Performing Arts and has given new salience to the arts in the republic's capital.

Most presidents, including even the two Roosevelts, remained rather indifferent to the physical appearance of the capital. Lafayette Square, in front of the White House, was surrounded by Federal row houses where once had lived notables like Dolley Madison and Stephen Decatur. The Eisenhower administration, seeking office space, had decided to replace the graceful old residences with banal modern office buildings. The Kennedys were appalled by the sentence of death pronounced on Lafayette Square.

"They are now planning to put up a hideous white modern court building," Jacqueline Kennedy wrote Bernard Boutin, the head of the General Services Administration. "The important thing is to preserve the 19th century feeling of Lafayette Square. . . . I so strongly feel that the White House should give the example in preserving our nation's past. Now we think of saving old buildings like Mt. Vernon and tear down everything in the 19th century—but, in the next hundred years, the 19th century will be of great interest and there will be none of it left; just plain glass skyscrapers."

After exhaustive discussions, Kennedy and William Walton, his architectural counselor, were about ready to give up the fight.

Mrs. Kennedy held out. "The wreckers haven't started yet," she said, "and until they do it can be saved." Then the president, running by chance into John Carl Warnecke, the San Francisco architect, asked his advice. Warnecke came up with a brilliant solution that protected the historic houses by placing new and harmonizing red-brick office buildings behind them.

The president kept careful watch on the progress of Lafayette Square. One day Walton apologized for interrupting him when weightier affairs were on his desk. "That's all right," the president said. "After all, this may be the only monument we'll leave."

The Eisenhower administration had also wanted to tear down the old State Department building, a charming Neoclassical structure with Baroque features erected just west of the White House during the Grant administration (and known today as the Old Executive Office Building). Jacqueline Kennedy saved that building too. "She was the one who really deserved the credit for the whole thing," Bernard Boutin recalled. "It was her idea. Her imagination. Her drive. Her ability to work with people." But when the new plan for Lafayette Square was unveiled, she whispered to Boutin, "Remember, not me. The president. The president, Bernie, the president." Boutin said, "She did not want to take any of the credit."

President Kennedy's great architectural dream was the rehabilitation of Pennsylvania Avenue, the broad boulevard running from the Capitol to the White House, conceived by Pierre Charles L'Enfant, the city's eighteenth-century planner, as the "grand axis" of the city but now decaying into block after block of dingy buildings and cheap shops. The Kennedys set up a Council on Pennsylvania Avenue, headed by the architect Nathaniel A. Owings and protected in the government by a brilliant and resourceful assistant secretary of labor named Daniel Patrick Moynihan.

"You, sir," said J. Roy Carroll Jr., president of the American Institute of Architects, to Kennedy in the spring of 1963, "are the first president of the United States—except, possibly, the first and third ones—who has had a vision of what architecture and its allied arts can mean to the people of the nation, and of what the careful nurturing of the architecture of the city of Washington can mean to the millions who come here to pay homage to the heart of their country."

On October 24, 1963, President Kennedy traveled north to Amherst College to take part in a ceremony honoring Robert Frost. "I see little of more importance to the future of our country and our civilization," Kennedy said, "than full recognition of the place of the artist. If art is to nourish the roots of our culture, society must set the artist free to follow his vision wherever it takes him. . . . The highest duty of the writer, the composer, the artist is to remain true to himself and to let the chips fall where they may. In serving his vision of the truth, the artist best serves his nation."

He concluded: "I look forward to an America which will not be afraid of grace and beauty, which will protect the beauty of our natural environment, which will preserve the great old American houses and squares and parks of our national past, and which will build handsome and balanced cities for our future. I look forward to an America which will reward achievement in the arts as we reward achievement in business or statecraft. I look forward to an America which will steadily raise the standards of artistic accomplishment and which will steadily enlarge cultural opportunities for all our citizens. And I look forward to an America which commands respect throughout the world not only for its strength but for its civilization as well."

The next month Goodwin, about to take over as White House special consultant on the arts, proposed to the president that the aesthetics of American society could be to him, and to his legacy, what the conservation of natural resources had been to Theodore Roosevelt. "It's a good idea," Kennedy said. "Let's work on it."

The next day the president departed for Dallas.

Much has been written about John and Jacqueline Kennedy; much has been imagined about them; their lives blend into legend, sometimes adoring, sometimes sensational, sometimes scurrilous. This is not the place for a comprehensive assessment of their thousand days in the White House. But the Kennedys must be given credit for the intensity of their commitment to the vitality of the arts in America.

In 1957 William Faulkner had told the American Academy of Arts and Letters, "The artist has no more actual place in the American culture of today than he has in the American economy of today, no place at all in the warp and woof, the thews and sinews, the mosaic of the American dream."

Seven years later, again before the Academy of Arts and Letters, Lewis Mumford called John Fitzgerald Kennedy "the first American president to give art, literature and music a place of dignity and honor in our national life." He should have added: in partnership with Jacqueline Bouvier Kennedy.

Opposite: Jacqueline Kennedy looking at the model for Lafayette Square with Bernard Boutin (at far left), head of the General Services Administration, and John Carl Warnecke, architect for the project. The square, in front of the White House, was redesigned to preserve its nineteenth-century feeling.

Jacqueline Bouvier Kennedy: A Reminiscence

Rachel Lambert Mellon

One summer day in the early 1960s Jacqueline Kennedy was in a drugstore not far from the village of Osterville, on Cape Cod, where we lived at the time. It was the perfect country drugstore, with a soda fountain on one side, Band-Aids, drugs, bathing caps, etc., in the middle, and a magazine stand at the far end. Here people gathered and picked up magazines to read before buying them. This morning there were more people than usual reading in intense silence.

When I walked in, I found Mrs. Kennedy sitting at the soda fountain, enjoying a large cone of peach ice cream, with five small children who were chattering away like happy sparrows. Seeing me, she called "Well hi!," and smiled mischievously. Looking over toward the magazine stand, which had her picture or some reference to her on many of the covers, she said, "all those people over there are so happy reading what I don't do, they have never looked over here to see what I really do." The truth of this remark has often been repeated in my mind when I hear and read the made-up, untrue fantasies about Mrs. Kennedy, whose charm in reality was simplicity.

We had met years before when she came with Adele Astaire Douglas and some friends from Washington for tea in my home in Virginia. That evening Dellie called and said, "young Mrs. Kennedy wants to call you, but feels I should ask you first if she should." Her telephone call the next morning was about her house. "I loved your house, but I don't like mine." She had noticed almost every detail with enthusiasm, but it was not until she said "I even loved the stale candies in the antique jars" that she won me over. I agreed to go to Washington and see if I could help. When I arrived, she was sitting on the floor surrounded by large books of maps and drawings. Her voice low, but with the unique charm that was one of her characteristics, she thanked me enthusiastically for coming. Mrs. Kennedy told me that the things she had loved most were the painted floors that I had found in Sweden and was able to duplicate at our Virginia farm.

Before we went much further, the front door opened and a large pram was bumped up the steps and into the front hall. "That's Caroline," she said smiling, and jumped up to carry the baby in to meet me. Before leaving, I understood her need for warmth in her house and the unusual details that would create it. More important, it was the beginning of a friendship that brought us both continuous joy.

Mrs. Kennedy was a true "bluestocking" in the old-fashioned sense of the word. She explored history in all its aspects and was fascinated when meeting people unlike herself, whose lives had created worlds unknown to her; however, it was her family and children who were foremost. This private world she guarded ceaselessly with dignity.

It was in mid-August of 1960, when, arriving home from Europe, I found three urgent phone messages waiting: "Please call Mrs. Kennedy." There was a seriousness in her voice, and when I called, she asked, "When can I come over?" She arrived a few hours later and, with short gasps for breath, told me, "Jack may be president. The count isn't in but what will I do?—that big house and all those curtains." Her fear of this enormous change in her life had focused on her house, her family, and her children.

Time passed, November came, the narrow margins of votes were counted, and Senator Kennedy had won.

John was born fifty-six days before the inauguration, and Mrs. Kennedy, in spite of a weakened back, had found her own way to this new life before it began. Her sense of history had helped her see the White House in a different way. It was the president's house, a large southern mansion, with an ever-changing atmosphere of administrations and new families that moved in and out. She studied its history, and with her youth, love of family, and love of life, worked endlessly to blend the past with the present.

She did not like it or feel that the title "first lady" was appropriate; she would be the president's wife. It was a big task she had to face—like exploring a new world. Fortunately, there existed the most unusual and wonderful man, Mr. J. B. West.

Opposite: The Jacqueline Kennedy Garden, designed by Rachel Lambert Mellon and dedicated by Mrs. Lyndon B. Johnson on April 22, 1965

He was the chief usher in the White House, a title that meant he knew all the intricacies of staff management, the ways of past families, the protocol, and the tiresome details. His fame lay in his way of dealing and working with people of all types and walks of life. His smile and calm never left him. Jacqueline Kennedy and I often wondered what would really shake Mr. West. I worked with him, not only helping her inside the White House but also with garden questions. Going to his office, I marveled at his almost empty desk. Mr. West was the president's young wife's greatest support and help from beginning to end. He was also the true friend of Mrs. Kennedy's secretary and school classmate, Nancy Tuckerman. Jacqueline Kennedy reached out to many friends and people, but it was the few close to her who helped her daily to find in the White House the understanding and sense of home she had had in Georgetown.

During the years Mrs. Kennedy was in the White House, she had three priorities that filled most of her time: her admiration for and support of the president, her time spent with the children, and bringing the fresh history and importance of the White House, as well as the lives of past presidents, to the children and people of America. The tours and White House guidebook are the results of her dreams and effort.

Jacqueline Kennedy was true to herself. Her gift of insight into people and her dislike of false pretenses were strong guidelines in carrying out her new responsibilities.

She dressed most of the time in pants and sweaters, with her tumbled hair often tied in a scarf, and radiated an irresistible smile. Nevertheless, she gave importance to her formal clothes in her role as the president's wife. Whatever she wore, she had her own sense of effortless elegance.

Her perception of the White House as a large southern mansion helped her make changes almost immediately, winning over sympathetic members of the devoted White House staff with her directness and sense of fairness. Windows were soon opened. Fireplaces and chimneys were cleaned so fires could burn in all the rooms when needed. She redesigned the flower room and the way flowers were to be arranged in all the State Rooms. Dozens of long-stem roses, which constantly arrived as gifts, were cut shorter and often mixed with country flowers. A new atmosphere blew through the White House like wind with a clearing sky. Cupboards and warehouses were opened to search for historic treasures. Entertaining was full of pleasure and celebrated the importance of the guests. The kitchen staff was changed and mixed American dishes with those of France. The existing party dining chairs were sad, not suitable for the new cheerfulness of the dining room, painted in white and gold. Traditional chairs used in Paris for such occasions were ordered and made in France.

She felt that the early influence of French culture on the new republic, introduced by George Washington and Thomas Jefferson, should be emphasized whenever possible in literature, social behavior, and taste. Washington's copious correspondence with Lafayette dealt with all subjects, including the exchange of seeds and plants with France. After Jefferson visited Paris, he, too, saw the importance of America's need to learn from this European country. Today, the gardens of Mount Vernon and Monticello continue to grow with their inspiration.

President Kennedy asked me to redesign the Rose Garden. He explained that after his trip to Europe, where he had met with the heads of state in Germany and France, he became aware of how walking in the gardens between serious meetings and lunch brought a common interest of the different nations together in a relaxed and informal way. The president was an active participant in the construction of the garden and had constant pleasure as it grew. Noticing a boxwood bush that looked not too well, he asked me how much it would cost to replace it. I told him, and he reached in his pocket and gave me the sum, explaining with a smile that he did not want to add it to the government's expense.

The Rose Garden was supervised and planted by a devoted and extraordinary man, Irwin Williams, who is still there after forty years. We met when he was in charge of Dangerfield Island, on the Potomac River, and, like Mr. West, he was the Kennedys' and my loyal and dear outdoor friend, forgiving dogs and ponies for trespassing and redoing the damage without a word.

I was in Antigua when news came over the radio from Martinique of the tragedy in Texas. We had no telephones on the island at the time to get further information. The earliest plane leaving Antigua was the next day. Arriving in New York the following evening, I found a message from Mr. West that Mrs. Kennedy wanted me to come to Washington. It was a stormy night when I left. I arrived at the North Portico of the White House at 2:00 a.m. The steps were lined with Marines. They clicked their heels as I passed, going up alone. Mr. West opened the door, he was alone; he had been sitting nearby waiting for my arrival. After embracing me, he said, with tears in his eyes, "Mrs. Kennedy is asleep now, but would like for you to be at the Capitol tomorrow morning at 9:00 to organize the flowers." I asked him if I could go in and pay my respects to the president. The East Room seemed particularly large. It was lit with candles. The chandeliers were draped in black gauze. In the center of the room lay the president under a large American flag. At each corner of the casket stood a motionless guard from each of the four services, Army, Navy, Air Force, and Marines. Holding tight to Mr. West's hand, I said my prayers.

We walked back together to the front door. As we went down the steps outside, a heavy snow was falling. The ground was already white. Three days later Mrs. Kennedy asked me if I would go to the Rose Garden and pick a small basket of remaining flowers. She handed me a note she had written, "Please put this in the basket for me and take it to Arlington."

Opposite, top: President Kennedy giving Princess Beatrix of the Netherlands a tour of the Rose Garden, April 18, 1963; bottom: White House flower arrangements. This page: Rachel Lambert Mellon, designer of the Rose Garden, photographed by Horst P. Horst for the February 1967 issue of *Vogue* magazine

Defining Style: Jacqueline Kennedy's White House Years

Hamish Bowles

As first lady, Jacqueline Bouvier Kennedy revolutionized the taste of the nation. Not only did she promote culture and the arts at the highest levels, she also brought to the public's awareness a discriminating style and an expertise in fashion, decorating, and entertaining. In so doing, as Carl Sferrazza Anthony, biographer of first ladies, wrote, she became "a symbol of the liberation from the notion that America had to be bourgeois." While the Trumans and the Eisenhowers had projected an air of cozy domesticity and espoused America's middlebrow cultural preferences, the Kennedys, as *Life* magazine noted, "consistently asserted a broad interest in artistic and intellectual distinction."

Jacqueline Kennedy's image as first lady was as carefully constructed as the stage that she set for her husband's presidency in her scrupulous restoration of the White House. Her personal taste gracefully spanned the divide that separated 1950s America from John F. Kennedy's New Frontier. She was at once a paradigm of old-fashioned dignity, sharing with her husband a love of history and a keen appreciation of ceremony, and a reluctant pop-culture icon, who, like John F. Kennedy, had an intuitive understanding of the power of image in an age when television was becoming a potent medium.

As Diana Vreeland, her valued friend and fashion mentor, expressed it in her 1984 autobiography, *D.V.*, Jacqueline Kennedy "put a little style into the White House and into being First Lady of the land, and *suddenly* 'good taste' became good taste. Before the Kennedys, good taste was never the point of modern America—at all. . . . The Kennedys released a positive attitude toward culture, toward style . . . and, since then, we've never gone back."

At the White House Jacqueline Kennedy turned state receptions into gala events, creating an atmosphere that enchanted her guests. Leonard Bernstein, remembering the dinner given for the governor of Puerto Rico—at which the great cellist Pablo Casals played—said that "when the moment comes for you to meet the President and First Lady, two ravishing people appear in the doorway who couldn't be more charming if they tried, who make you feel utterly welcome, even with a huge gathering. . . . The food is marvelous, the wines are delicious . . . people are laughing, laughing out loud . . . I've never seen so many happy artists in my life. It was a joy to watch it."

An accomplished linguist with a degree in French literature, Jacqueline Kennedy "loved everything French, the history, the literature, the food, and always had," remembers her sister, Lee Radziwill. "Louise de La Vallière [Louis XIV's mistress] and Madame de La Fayette [the seventeenth-century novelist and author of *La Princesse de Clèves*] were her heroines. She had a great knowledge of French history and a great sense of history." Her elegant Continental tastes were revealed in her fashion, decorating, and cultural interests. She had an eager curiosity, screening foreign films for more intimate White House gatherings, and "was very much the erudite reader," as her friend and fellow connoisseur Jayne Wrightsman recalls. "She finished as many as eight to ten books a week, on subjects of architecture, history, and biography."

Jacqueline Kennedy also had a keen understanding of the semantics of dress and of the ways in which she could use her public image to help communicate the more abstract ideals that were important to her. In projecting a vision of dynamic modern elegance, she provided a potent counterpoint to the tenets of the Kennedy administration, with its youthful idealism, ardent internationalism, and striving for social change.

The results of Jacqueline Kennedy's image projection had an unexpected impact not only on the fashion industry at home and abroad but also on the nation's philosophy of style. By March 1961 *Women's Wear Daily* noted that the "Jackie look" had become "part of the retail ad language," and *Ladies' Home Journal* wrote that "Jackie's slightest fashion whim triggers seismic tremors up and down Seventh Avenue." Her influence crossed what were then clearly defined generational divides.

Opposite: Pre-inaugural portrait of Jacqueline Kennedy, charcoal drawing by artist René Bouché for *Vogue* magazine's February 1961 issue

At Manhattan's Easter Parade in 1962, fashion writer Eugenia Sheppard reported, "there were half a million Jackies on the street, all teen age and under."

Meticulous attention to detail was the keynote of Mrs. Kennedy's approach to the projects that absorbed her as first lady. Her social secretary, Letitia Baldrige (who had worked for Ambassador Clare Boothe Luce in Rome and Ambassador David Bruce and his stylish wife, Evangeline, in Paris), recalled in a 1964 oral history recorded for the Kennedy Library that "a great professional sense of organization was immediately apparent. . . . here was an organized mind and a very efficient mind."

Jacqueline Kennedy proved adept at seeking out experts in all the areas that interested her and at orchestrating their efforts with winning charm and her own perfectionism. "You can't do it all by yourself, so you must pick the people you know who are qualified for each field and tell them what [it is] you wish," she once said—"and supervise it all, as nothing is ever any good without [the] overall unified supervision of the person who is putting all this in motion." She rigorously oversaw her own visual presentation. Working with her favored American designer, Oleg Cassini, and his team, along with her other fashion resources, her hairdresser, Kenneth Battelle, and Roy Halston Frowick and the millinery department of Bergdorf Goodman, she created an image that blended her informed tastes in fashion with the gravitas of her new role. "I will never become stuffy," she wrote to Cassini, "but there is a dignity to the office that suddenly hits one." Lee Radziwill notes that "she had a great sense of what was appropriate—and of what the public wants of you, because that's who you're pleasing."

After the presidential election, Jacqueline Kennedy said, "I feel as though I had just turned into a piece of public property. It's really frightening to lose your anonymity at thirty-one." As first lady, therefore, she used her wardrobe of "state clothing," as she characterized it, as a shield and style as an effective weapon. J. B. West, the White House chief usher, an invaluable friend and ally in every aspect of the management and restoration of the executive mansion, observed that when she "was performing with such grace and authority the role of First Lady . . . I thought of her as an actress." Her official clothing, both at home and on the world stage, was a vital element in this role-playing.

Similarly, Queen Elizabeth II had worked with her court dressmakers, the romanticist Norman Hartnell and the more pragmatic designer Hardy Amies, to establish the guidelines for her own image: silhouettes were defined; colors were clear, bright, and pure, so that she could be spotted easily in a crowd; hats did not cover the face that the public had come to see. Although Jacqueline Kennedy absorbed some of these ideas into the creation of her own public wardrobe, her clothes were informed with an understated modern elegance, characterized by clean lines, solid colors, and ease of movement.

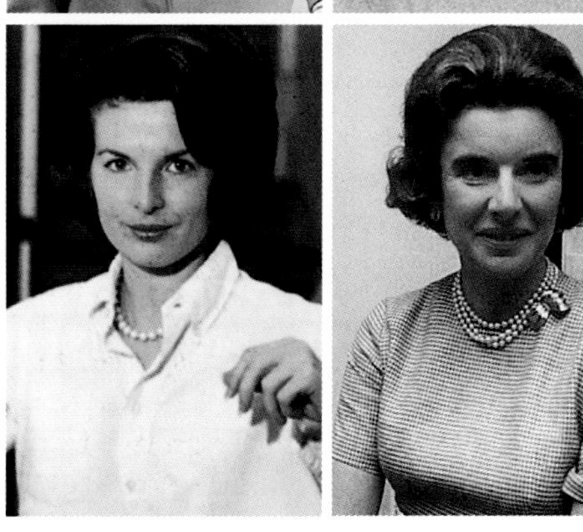

For her appearances abroad Jacqueline Kennedy used her intelligence and style to give further weight and luster to her husband's presidency; in so doing, she helped change the world's view of America. For the first lady's official and semiofficial tours "every country was a campaign," as Oleg Cassini noted, with clothing an essential element in the battle plan. "It was proper that she, a young and beautiful woman," wrote Pearl S. Buck, the Nobel Prize–winning author, "should so represent our nation that Americans could take pride in her appearance as well as in her behavior." As John Fairchild, editor of *Women's Wear Daily,* wrote, "she influenced the women of the world to look and feel better." And her influence was universal. "It was epidemic, that wardrobe," noted first lady Betty Ford, and the newly crowned Miss America sighed, "if only I looked like Jackie." During Mrs. Kennedy's 1961 visit to England, the London *Times* put

Jean Shrimpton in a dark wig to illustrate the phenomenon of the "Jackie look," and milliners worked overtime to make pillbox hats. The Russian magazine *Mody* featured advertisements for clothes with the "Jackie look," and the Polish magazine *Swait* affirmed that "Jackie has entered the group of a few women in the world who, today, as in times past, set the style and tone of their epoch. . . . the face and silhouette of Jackie are known to people all over the civilized world."

In the years following World War II, socially prominent women of great personal style, such as Babe Paley, Gloria Guinness, and C.Z. Guest, had the subtle nuances of their tastes in fashion, decorating, and entertaining scrutinized in elitist magazines such as *Harper's Bazaar, Vogue,* and *Town and Country,* yet their influence remained limited to their own sequestered worlds. Instead, the potent appeal of movies, television, and popular music guided the way women wanted to look and behave. Jacqueline Kennedy transformed this dynamic. She succeeded in "redeeming fashion from the puritan ethic of sin," wrote Marilyn Bender of the New York *Times* (in *The Beautiful People,* 1967).

Although her background was patrician, Jacqueline Kennedy's appeal was popular. Bernard Roshco noted in *The Rag Race* (1963) that Mrs. Kennedy "has been responsible for bringing to the widest public the understated look. This look is one that 'til now has been a strictly upperclass fashion." She headed the Best Dressed list for four years, was inducted into the fashion Hall of Fame in 1965, and was cited for her "symbol of fashion leadership to the average woman everywhere."

By the time she joined her husband on the presidential campaign, Jacqueline Kennedy had clearly laid the foundations for the visual presentation that she would build on as first lady—a reductive elegance that ensured her clothing would remain a quiet foil to her personality. Her informal clothing, however, revealed a very different and maverick aspect. During the campaign her "devil-may-care chic," as the New York *Times* described it, came under relentless scrutiny. On September 11, 1960, the *Times* magazine fashion writer Martha Weinman reported that "when Jacqueline Kennedy, then five days the wife of a Presidential nominee, stepped aboard the family yacht in Hyannis Port, Massachusetts, wearing an orange pullover sweater, shocking pink Capri pants and a *bouffant* hairdo that gamboled merrily in the breeze, even those newsmen present who could not tell shocking pink from Windsor Rose knew they were witnessing something of possibly vast political consequence." Her carefree youthful style was a counterpart to her husband's athleticism. In Jacqueline Kennedy's case this blithe elegance might have been a response to her mother's more strictly controlled taste.

Janet Lee Auchincloss set exacting standards for her Bouvier daughters. They were brought up with the manners of a generation trained to write gracious thank-you notes, to appreciate the subtle arts of the great hostess and the management of large households, and to observe correct formality of dress. It was a time, as writer Peggy Noonan later noted, "when elegance was a kind of statement, a way of dressing up the world, and so a generous act." In the custom of the time and milieu, Janet Auchincloss largely prescribed her elder daughter's sartorial choices; she even chose her wedding gown, an uncharacteristically elaborate confection by the African-American dressmaker Anne Lowe, who was celebrated for her painstaking dressmaking effects and unrestrained use of applied decoration.

"I flatter myself on being able at times to walk out of the house looking like a poor man's Paris copy," Jacqueline Bouvier wrote in the autobiography that she submitted for *Vogue*'s 1951 Prix de Paris, "but often my mother will run up to inform me

Opposite, top: The "Jackie look," photographed by Yale Joel for *Time* magazine, 1961; bottom: The first lady's support team included (clockwise from top left) Letitia Baldrige, J.B. West, Nancy Tuckerman, and Pamela Turnure. This page, top: Jacqueline Kennedy's contemporary elegance, photographed at a 1961 White House reception; bottom: Jacqueline Kennedy in Hyannis Port, 1960

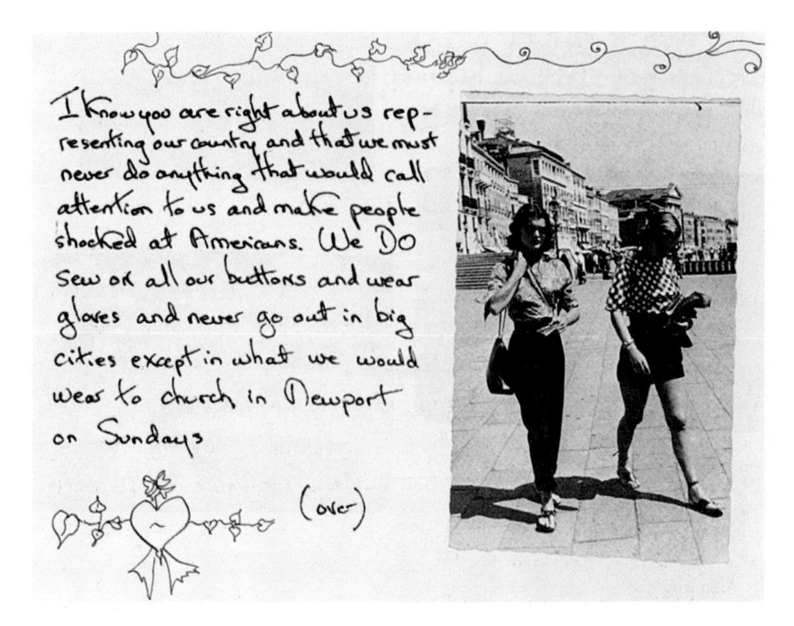

that my left stocking is crooked or the right-hand top button about to fall off. This I realize, is the Unforgivable Sin."

The Bouvier sisters, however, were not above playful irreverence. They spent the summer of 1951 traveling through Europe on a pilgrimage to meet the art historian Bernard Berenson (with whom Lee had been corresponding) and prepared a scrapbook diary as a record for their mother, illustrated with tales of their adventures (published by Delacorte Press in 1974 as *One Special Summer*). "I know you are right about us representing our country and that we must never do anything that would call attention to us and make people shocked at Americans," Lee Bouvier wrote. "We DO sew on all our buttons and wear gloves and never go out in big cities except in what we would wear to church in Newport on Sundays." As an ironic footnote, the sisters placed a snapshot of themselves in Venice next to this text; both are gloveless and stockingless in sandals and sunglasses; Lee Bouvier wears shorts, Jacqueline, prefiguring her later preference for Pucci and Galitzine capri pants, wears tapered slacks.

The Bouvier sisters often patronized local Newport and Washington dressmakers, establishing a pattern of personal involvement in the design of their clothes. The Georgetown dressmaker Mini Rhea made items for their mother and her circle. In a pattern that she repeated as first lady in her relationship with Oleg Cassini's studio, Jacqueline Bouvier brought Rhea her own "squiggled dress designs," as well as French fashion magazines, for inspiration. Writing in 1962, Rhea remembered that her stylish young client "had a perfect horror of overdressing. . . . Jackie, even then, insisted on cleaner, neater, more compact lines and material with firmer body, so that the garments would hold their shape. . . . All of the fashions which Jackie has favored have suddenly become high fashion."

In 1951 the twenty-one-year-old Jacqueline Bouvier, then a senior at George Washington University, proved how sophisticated her fashion sensibility was when she entered *Vogue*'s Prix de Paris, a competition that the magazine established to "dissolve the 'no experience' barrier that exists between the young and the professional world." The playful self-portrait, sharply observed essays, knowing style references, and heady fashion critiques she submitted suggested her worldly tastes and pointed to her love of history. They also ensured that she won first prize in a field of more than a thousand college seniors. When asked to submit a concept for an issue of *Vogue*, she chose the theme of "Nostalgia," which, she maintained, "can add a grace and a nuance to our living and to our clothes when it is hinted at occasionally and good-naturedly."

Throughout the 1950s the output of Seventh Avenue was largely predicated on the dictates of Paris haute couture. As late as 1968 fashion historian Robert Riley wrote that "the majority of manufacturers and retailers still look to Paris for the Law and Covenant of Chic." The work of designers Gabrielle (Coco) Chanel and Hubert de Givenchy was closest to Jacqueline Kennedy's emerging fashion aesthetic in the 1950s and continued to shape her style as first lady. Chanel had closed down her couture house at the outbreak of the war but was so appalled by the exaggerated fashions of the emerging postwar couturiers ("Men make clothes in which one can't move") that in 1954 she decided to reopen it. Although the French fashion press eviscerated her collection, influential American editors felt that the clothes suited the needs of American women who wanted easy formality without discomfort. Their proselytizing helped to reestablish Chanel's influence, which was soon reflected at all levels of the American fashion industry, from

Norman Norell (who created a collection in homage to the designer) to the suit and coat manufacturer Davidow. In many ways Jacqueline Kennedy was the paradigm of the Chanel client. Chanel's clothes, fitted lightly to skim the body, were designed with a sense of comfort and ease that nevertheless did not deny their couture status. As first lady, she continued to wear the Chanel clothes that she already owned and to order Chanel originals through Saks and from Paris via her friend and fashion scout Letizia Mowinckel.

During the 1950s, however, Jacqueline Kennedy's style most clearly followed the trajectory of Givenchy's designing career. Givenchy had made a name for himself designing playful and inventive clothes for Elsa Schiaparelli's boutique. His own house was an immediate success when it opened in 1952. He presented youthful garments, often in humble cottons and in interchangeable pieces, that redefined the nature of couture, until then largely responding to the needs of a mature, worldly clientele. A year later, however, Givenchy experienced a personal and professional epiphany when he met Cristobal Balenciaga, then acknowledged as the greatest designer of the day. As friend and mentor, Balenciaga redefined Givenchy's approach.

Givenchy's new line blended his mentor's austere Spanish aesthetic with his own lighthearted French tastes. For many elegant young Americans the luxurious simplicity of Givenchy's clothes and the exposure that they received through his symbiotic muse, Audrey Hepburn (whom he had been dressing since the 1954 movie *Sabrina*), made him the Parisian couturier of choice. For Jacqueline Kennedy Givenchy's reductive approach was appealing, for it disguised subtleties of construction that appealed to her connoisseur's eye but remained deceptively simple enough to emphasize the wearer rather than the garment. Siriol Hugh-Jones characterized Jacqueline Kennedy's style for *Town and Country* in July 1962 as "the look that fashion magazines, with awful perseverance, used to call uncluttered and that gives the impression that after fully dressing someone has neatened you up with a sharp razor blade and finished off the whole effect with a small mathematical bow."

Jacqueline Kennedy also bought American-made versions of original Paris models, either from the custom departments of stores such as Bergdorf Goodman or, more inexpensively, from Ohrbach's. For a Wild West ball at the Plaza Hotel in 1959, she wore what was probably an Ohrbach's copy of a short Givenchy evening dress with a puffball hem and a daring swimsuit back. For such a flamboyant dress it made sense to choose an inexpensive Ohrbach's interpretation, but for the highly edited wardrobe that she assembled during the campaign, she preferred beautifully made French pieces. "My clothes really take hard work—so they will have to be well made," she later wrote to Diana Vreeland.

At this time Jacqueline Kennedy was developing her style in other areas and establishing professional

Opposite, top: Jacqueline and Lee Bouvier in Venice, 1951; bottom: *Vogue*'s Prix de Paris winner, Jacqueline Bouvier, photographed by Richard Rutledge, 1951. This page, top: An American-made Pierre Balmain–inspired ball gown, worn by Jacqueline Kennedy for a portrait by Yousuf Karsh, 1957; bottom: Hubert de Givenchy, photographed by Mark Shaw, ca. 1956. As first lady, Jacqueline Kennedy continued to wear these clothes from Givenchy's 1959 collections.

collaborations and friendships that would continue to flourish at the White House. She numbered among her close circle of friends women of commanding personal taste, such as the distinguished horticulturist and landscape gardener Rachel Lambert Mellon. Mrs. Mellon suggested that the White House be restored in the spirit of a Southern country mansion and worked to breathe life and atmosphere into the interiors. In a gesture that owed a debt to Mrs. Mellon's assured style, the White House's lugubrious Victorian palms were replaced with topiary trees in Versailles tubs.

Her influence had its most enduring impact on the White House grounds. At the president's request she redesigned the Rose Garden, which had been planned originally by John Adams in 1800, landscaped later by Thomas Jefferson, and named by the first Mrs. Woodrow Wilson in 1913. Mrs. Mellon's layout displayed great flair and elegance. In the manner of an early American garden, she extended the lawn and framed it with a trellis of low boxwood hedges, anchored with pink magnolia Alexandria in each corner and centered with crab apple trees. The White House chief floral designer Elmer (Rusty) M. Young and his staff created the arrangements that the first lady favored, combining "old Dutch still life paintings with naturalness." Mrs. Kennedy banished gladioli and hothouse roses and insisted "that flowers of the season be used so that the impression is that they come out of the garden (although they don't) when possible." Seventeenth-century Dutch manuals from Mrs. Mellon's unique library of botanical and horticultural books were consulted.

Mrs. Mellon introduced the socially well-connected decorator Sister (Dorothy) Parish to Jacqueline Kennedy. The Kennedys' elegant Georgetown house, with its assured mix of eighteenth-century French antiques and fresh-sprigged chintzes, had been decorated with Parish's help and reflected the unforced coziness of her signature look. "If my Undecorated look has meant rooms that are personal, comfortable, friendly and gay," Sister Parish once declared, "I feel I have accomplished a great deal."

The first lady enlisted Sister Parish's help in the restoration of the White House, where her influence was particularly expressed in the redecoration of the second-floor family rooms. In these informal apartments she introduced homespun touches that reflected the charm of the Kennedys' Georgetown house, providing continuity and familiarity for their young family and offsetting what Jacqueline Kennedy characterized as the "interior remoteness" of the White House.

As a child of eleven, according to family friend Mary Thayer, Jacqueline Bouvier had visited the White House for the first time and had been dismayed to find so few historical furnishings or even a guidebook. In December 1960, during her tour of her new home with Mamie Eisenhower, she discovered that this sorry state of affairs still prevailed. She told John Walker, the director of the National Gallery of Art, Washington, that it looked like Lubianka, the notorious Soviet prison. Later, in spring of 1963, in response to questions posed by the journalist Frances Lewine, she noted more diplomatically: "I've always cared about old houses, about preserving the past. In Georgetown and Newport, where I lived—I was always sad when an old building was torn down to make way for a parking lot. When I learned we would be living in the White House, how could I help but think of restoring as much of its past as possible. It would have seemed to me criminal not to—and I cared terribly about it. Here is a house that all Americans love and practically revere—and practically nothing in it earlier than 1948. . . . In the days before the Inauguration and for weeks afterwards I read everything I could find in the Library of Congress on the White House past."

Mrs. Kennedy's restoration of the White House was to go far beyond her aesthetic preferences, as she made clear in a rare interview for *Life* magazine (September 1961). "Everything in the White House must have a reason for being there," she said. "It would be a sacrilege merely to 'redecorate' it—a word I hate. It must be *restored*—and that has nothing to do with decoration. That is a question of scholarship."

After Jacqueline Kennedy's visit with Mrs. Eisenhower, J.B. West sent her an album of photographs of the mansion's rooms as they were in 1950 under Truman and again in 1960 under Eisenhower. Their undistinguished paintings and department-store furnishings, dreary colors, and bland arrangements of flowers and succulents suggested the tremendous work that lay ahead. Jacqueline Kennedy passed the album on to Sister Parish, with her instructions attached. "I want our private quarters to be heaven for us naturally," she wrote, "but use as much of their stuff as possible + buy as little new—as I want to spend lots of my budget below in the public rooms—which people see + will do you and I proud!" The Lincoln Bedroom, with its historically appropriate furnishings, was "the only room in the whole place I like—we can't change it—wouldn't want to."

Shortly after the inauguration Jacqueline Kennedy met with David Finley, the chairman of the Fine Arts Commission. Their discussions led to the establishment of the Fine Arts Committee for the White House (see Schlesinger essay, pp. 3–11). She persuaded Henry Francis du Pont, founder of the Winterthur Museum, near Wilmington, Delaware, and a renowned collector of eighteenth- and early-nineteenth-century American furnishings and decorative arts, to serve as chairman of her committee. The appointment affirmed the credibility of the project and its apolitical ends (du Pont, like several of the committee members, was a staunch Republican).

Mrs. Kennedy set about recruiting socially prominent collectors and philanthropists, as well as leading museum directors and curators, to aid her in implementing her ambitious restoration plans. The first lady could not ask Congress for the necessary funds, and thus, as she noted, "the task ahead seemed Herculean if not impossible." Mrs. Kennedy proved particularly adept at beguiling potential donors, however, and the publicity generated by her efforts led to an avalanche of donations, some very significant, from citizens around the country. On July 4, 1961, the White House announced that these gifts would be the foundation for a museum that would be a "testimonial to American fine arts and cabinetmaking."

In the fall of 1961 the Special Committee for White House Paintings was formed under the chairmanship of James W. Fosburgh, of the Frick Collection, New York. Its mandate was to acquire a permanent collection of works by eighteenth- and nineteenth-century American artists, as well as portraits (ideally from life) of the presidents and first ladies to replace copies then hanging on the mansion's walls. The first important work thus acquired was a superb portrait of Benjamin Franklin by the Scottish artist David Martin, painted from life in Paris in 1767 and donated by Mr. and Mrs. Walter Annenberg. The collection eventually included important American paintings, such as Rubens Peale's meticulous *Still Life with Fruit* (1862) and Childe Hassam's *The Avenue in the Rain* (1917).

Realizing the need for a museum professional to care for the growing collection, Jacqueline Kennedy appointed the first curator for the White House, Lorraine Waxman Pearce. A 1958 graduate of the Winterthur program of studies in early American

Opposite, top: Jacqueline Kennedy with Baroness de la Bovillerie at a Wild West ball at the Plaza Hotel, December 8, 1959. Her pink dress was an American copy of Givenchy's fall–winter 1958 model number 2323, shown to its left; bottom: Sister Parish and her associate designer, Albert Hadley, photographed for *House and Garden* by Christian Reinhardt. This page: The Solarium in the White House, as decorated by the Eisenhowers, 1960

culture, Pearce's research on the early-nineteenth-century French-born New York cabinetmaker Charles-Honoré Lannuier led to the acquisition of several examples of his furniture, among them his exquisite marble-inlaid *guéridon* (circular table), a prominent feature of the Red Room. Other master craftsmen whose work was sought by the new Fine Arts Committee and ultimately acquired included Duncan Phyfe, Joseph Burgess of Baltimore, and John Shaw of Annapolis. Pearce was also instrumental in preparing the text for *The White House: An Historic Guide,* the inception of which is discussed in the essay by Arthur M. Schlesinger Jr. in this volume. Pearce was succeeded in 1962 by William Voss Elder III, originally the registrar; in October 1963, Elder was replaced by James Roe Ketchum.

Jacqueline Kennedy also initiated a bill to ensure that White House objects could not be deaccessioned as had been the pattern in the past. Prior to the Kennedy administration White House furnishings were not protected in any way. One of the casualties was the State Dining Room fireplace, installed by President Theodore Roosevelt as part of the McKim, Mead and White renovations of 1902, which disappeared during the Truman administration. In September 1961 the White House received official museum status through an act of Congress, with the Smithsonian Institution as the watchdog. The first lady noted that such vigilance was necessary "so that nothing—no matter of how little value—would ever be sold or thrown away again."

While the Fine Arts Committee was energetically seeking donations of furniture and decorative objects for the White House, Jacqueline Kennedy was also coordinating the efforts of her interior designers for the intended settings for these pieces. Jayne Wrightsman, with her unparalleled contacts in the realm of fine and decorative arts and her knowledge of the highly specialized world of collectors and dealers, proved an invaluable friend, committee member, and motivator of the White House project, bringing to it her own refined taste, scholarship, and benevolence. Mrs. Wrightsman had arranged for her distinguished decorator, Stéphane Boudin, of Jansen of Paris, to visit and advise Jacqueline Kennedy on her Georgetown home in the spring of 1959. Here, as he later would in the White House, Boudin overlaid Parish's coziness with a sense of classical French rigor. Architectural historian John Cornforth considered Boudin "arguably the most brilliant historicist decorator in the years before and after the Second World War." Boudin also orchestrated the interiors of such exacting clients as the duke and duchess of Windsor, C.Z. and Winston Guest, and Nancy Lancaster. He had also worked with Ambassador Hervé and Nicole Alphand at the French Embassy in Washington. In addition to these prestigious private residential commissions, Boudin had undertaken museum projects, including Malmaison, the ravishing country retreat of Joséphine Bonaparte. "I can never ever thank you enough for twisting Boudin's arm and making that enchanting, brilliant man come to Washington," Jacqueline Kennedy wrote to Jayne Wrightsman after the Georgetown visit. "I think I learned as much as I have in all the years since I started caring about houses and pretty things—He counselled me against so many large expenditures I thought I should make—good dining chairs—bergères—Meissen tureens, ormolu candlesticks etc.—saying that they would be too pompous in their surroundings."

Mrs. Kennedy's admiration for Boudin's scholarship and taste later ensured that he would become the "primary visionary," as decorative arts historian James A. Abbott noted, of her restoration of the White House. The Jansen firm acted as antiques dealer and architect-decorator and was celebrated for its extensive historical archives and documents. While Sister Parish operated with a skeleton staff, Jansen employed six hundred and fifty craftspeople and an army of designers. The results were a testament to these extraordinary resources and to the symbiotic tastes of Mrs. Kennedy and Boudin.

Boudin's bravura concepts won him the enduring admiration of the first lady. "When you saw him work, you saw what no American decorator can do,"

Jacqueline Kennedy later said. "In France, you are trained as an interior architect, really. Boudin's eye for placement and proportion was absolutely right." Jacqueline Kennedy's collaboration with Boudin resulted in the transformation of the formal rooms—their schemes running a gamut of styles reflecting the personal tastes of the presidencies—from the fragile Jeffersonian Federal elegance of the Green Room to the imposing Victoriana of the Treaty Room. This approach ensured that the White House assumed the palimpsest character of a stately house, in which succeeding generations had left their various imprints. The Blue Room, underwritten by Charles and Jayne Wrightsman, and thus the purest expression of the tastes of Boudin and Mrs. Kennedy, "was the restoration's benchmark," noted James Abbott; it remained Jacqueline Kennedy's personal favorite. "The Blue Room is a formal reception room, and so you have a sense of state, ceremony, arrival and grandeur," she noted. "Boudin gave it that, and he did it so simply."

As restored, the Blue Room maintained the austere elegance of the French Empire style preferred by President James Monroe, who in 1817 ordered furniture made by the Parisian master craftsman Pierre-Antoine Bellangé. (Presidents Washington, Jefferson, and Madison also acquired French furnishings and objets d'art for the White House.) Jacqueline Kennedy's restoration highlighted both significant donations (including torchères from Malmaison donated by the Wrightsmans) and serendipitous rediscoveries such as Bellangé's giltwood pier table, which she found, thickly covered with gold radiator paint, languishing in the White House carpentry workshop. In a basement storeroom Mrs. Kennedy and Lorraine Pearce found the vermeil service that Monroe had also ordered from France in 1817 and that would be displayed in the Blue Room. A search of the ground-floor Broadcast Room turned up the desk made from the timbers of the H.M.S. *Resolute*, a gift from Queen Victoria to President Rutherford B. Hayes, which was placed in the Oval Office for President Kennedy's use. "By now I know every corner of the White House," Mrs. Kennedy told *Life* in the fall of 1961. "I poked into them all. It was exciting, a new mystery story every day."

Betty Monkman, the current White House curator, writes in her recently published book that Jacqueline Kennedy's "interest in history, aesthetic sense, organizational ability, and attention to detail led to a new way of thinking about the historic character of the house and the institutionalization of its museum role . . . Mrs. Kennedy's efforts in recapturing a sense of the nation's history in the context of the White House influenced historic houses and state governors' mansions and led to revival of interest in and new appreciation of American neoclassical furnishings of the period 1810–30. She set a standard for future refurbishing projects in the White House."

Jayne Wrightsman also acknowledges Jacqueline Kennedy's extraordinary commitment to the

Opposite, top: *Benjamin Franklin,* by the Scottish artist David Martin; bottom: Jacqueline Kennedy with Bellangé's pier table, photographed by Ed Clark. This page, top: Stéphane Boudin at the home of the Winston Guests, photographed by Henri Cartier-Bresson for *Vogue*, 1963; bottom: Jayne Wrightsman at home on Fifth Avenue, photographed by Cecil Beaton for *Vogue*, 1960

restoration. "Jackie had a terrific overall grasp, the idea of what the White House should be and a great sense of what was right for the State Rooms—whose proportions were so outlandish—she never stopped working for one second. Nothing was too much trouble. It was a miracle what she did in three years."

As President Kennedy said during the 1962 televised tour of the White House, during which the first lady revealed her work in progress, "Anything which dramatizes the great story of the United States—as I think the White House does—is worthy of the closest attention and respect by Americans who live here and who visit here and who are part of the citizenry. That's why I'm glad that Jackie is making the effort she's making."

Pride in the first lady's efforts was also reflected on a national level. *House and Garden* noted in July 1962 that the transformed White House represented "Washington's most inspiring example of the juxtaposition of charm and grandeur. . . . The care with which the White House has been restored and is now being made a shrine of elegance and historical associations has won the approval of the whole country."

In fashion, Jacqueline Kennedy, as first lady, succeeded in converting a nation to an appreciation of her refined and sophisticated Francophile tastes. While these had always been valued in the context of her social world, they had once proved politically hazardous for the wife of the Democratic presidential candidate and prompted a new trend in investigative fashion reporting. When John Fairchild took over the editorship of *Women's Wear Daily* in 1960, he set about transforming its existing editorial focus on garment-industry business news and adopting the more aggressive, gossipy tone championed by Eugenia Sheppard, the New York *Herald Tribune*'s women's-features editor. The newspaper's publisher, James Brady, wrote, "*WWD* was a profitable, respected, and obscure little trade newspaper in 1961 when John F. Kennedy came to the White House. . . . It was Jacqueline Kennedy who gave us our opening."

In *WWD*'s front-page editorial of July 13, 1960, Fairchild wrote, "Those smart and charming Kennedys—Jacqueline, wife of the senator, and his mother, Mrs. Joseph P., are running for election on the Paris Couture fashion ticket. . . . Together, the two Kennedys spend an estimated $30,000 per year for Paris clothes and hats—more than most United States professional buyers. . . . Jacqueline Kennedy orders mostly from sketches like a mail order catalogue—at Cardin, Grès, Givenchy, Balenciaga, Chanel and Bugnand. Each house has a well-shaped Jacqueline Kennedy dummy." The Associated Press picked up the story and compounded its sensationalism by suggesting that Fairchild's figure represented Jacqueline Kennedy's personal wardrobe expenditure. The New York *Times*'s Nan Robertson questioned Mrs. Kennedy about it and received the memorable response, "I couldn't spend that much unless I wore sable underwear."

The Republicans stepped swiftly into the fray. "I like American designers," Pat Nixon announced. "I think they are the best in the world. I buy most of my clothes off the racks in different stores around Washington."

Pat Nixon's Republican-cloth-coat frugality aside, there were even more pressing political reasons for the first lady to wear American-made clothes. Significant support for John F. Kennedy's presidential campaign had come from the International Ladies' Garment Workers' Union (ILGWU). Under the presidency of David Dubinsky, whom the *Times* called "the most imaginative and creative labor leader in America," the union had become a powerful lobbying force. "No one in the industry," wrote Phyllis Lee Levin in *The Wheels of Fashion* (1965), "no designer, manufacturer nor operator would not readily admit that Dubinsky was emperor and arbiter of American fashion."

The union had raised nearly $300,000 in contributions toward Kennedy's presidential campaign. "Wherever candidate Kennedy and his running mate travelled," its annual report noted, "they found ILGWU members in the forefront of the huge and enthusiastic crowds." The Seventh Avenue rally held by the ILGWU and the New York Liberal Party on October 27, 1960, drew an estimated quarter of a million people. The Liberal Party's four hundred thousand votes, the report added, "were decisive in Kennedy's carrying New York State—whose 45 electoral votes were crucial in determining the outcome of the election." Dubinsky lobbied John F. Kennedy on the issue of the first lady's unpatriotic wardrobe. Julius Hochman, director of the Union Label Department of the ILGWU, added his voice when he wrote to Eleanor Lambert, the doyenne of fashion publicists, who had been advising Jacqueline Kennedy and her office: "I think that you will do Mrs. Kennedy and the entire country a great service if you will convince Mrs. Kennedy that her Inauguration wardrobe be American made in every way."

Clockwise from top: The restored Blue Room in early 1963; transitional stage in the decoration of the Blue Room, showing the original Bellangé pier table that Mrs. Kennedy rediscovered and the Truman-era wall covering; the restored Red Room in early 1962, with the Lannuier table in front of the sofa

There was further political pressure from the milliners' union, led by Alex Rose, who also lobbied the president to persuade his wife to support their industry. She did, turning to the custom-millinery department of Bergdorf Goodman, where Halston was the designer. Jacqueline Kennedy coordinated her requirements with saleswoman Marita O'Connor and store couture director Ethel Frankau. Working with them, she established that oversize berets and domed pillbox hats of the type that Givenchy, Balenciaga, and Dior's Yves Saint Laurent had been producing a year or two earlier would suit her best. Again, she was not concerned with the latest fashion developments but with establishing the fundamentals of her style. Although hats now assumed importance, Jacqueline Kennedy's hairstyle continued to be a key element in the totality of her look. Her hairdresser, Kenneth Battelle, had first worked with Jacqueline Kennedy in 1954, when he was one of an army of stylists at Helena Rubinstein's Manhattan salon. Then, he remembers, Jacqueline Kennedy "had short hair that was rather curly and had a mind of its own," a gamine Audrey Hepburn look that Battelle encouraged her to grow out. He had big Lucite rollers especially made that gave her hair the lift of an "Italian cut," the template for the look that would endure throughout the White House years. Kenneth (as he came to be known) was summoned to work with Mrs. Kennedy for the inaugural ceremonies, and thereafter he made frequent trips to Washington for important state events.

As she had responded diplomatically to pressure from the millinery union without compromising her own aesthetic, Jacqueline Kennedy addressed the need to develop a wardrobe focused on the work of American designers. She turned for advice to Diana Vreeland, the hieratic and fantastically original fashion editor of *Harper's Bazaar*. In spite of Mrs. Vreeland's decidedly French instincts, she covered the American fashion market for the magazine. Bettina Ballard, her opposite number at *Vogue*, admired her "oracular approach to fashion" and willingly conceded that she was "the one person in the American fashion field who understands with every bone in her body what the word *elegant* really means."

With her every fashion purchase scrupulously, but often inaccurately, recorded by the fashion press, there was clearly a need for Jacqueline Kennedy to focus on a limited field of designers. Mamie Eisenhower had relied almost exclusively on Mollie Parnis, whose prim and elaborate clothes (along with Sally Victor's hats and Trifari's costume jewelry) came to define her style. On August 1, 1960, Diana Vreeland received a ten-page handwritten letter from the first lady, asking her advice to help "solve an enormous problem which is clothes! . . . I must start to buy American clothes and have it known where I buy them—my own little Mollie Parnis! There have been several newspaper stories and lots of letters—about me wearing Paris clothes, and Mrs. Nixon running up hers on the sewing machine. . . . Just remember I like terribly simple, covered up clothes," she added—"the nearest to Balenciaga & Givenchy" or "Chanel velvet suits." And, she noted firmly, "I hate prints."

She expressed concern that the pieces she had seen published by some of the preeminent American evening-wear

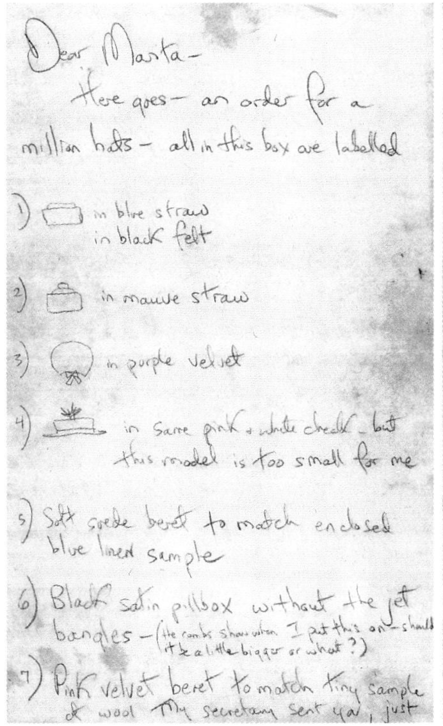
Dear Marita—
Here goes— an order for a million hats— all in this box are labelled

1) in blue straw
in black felt

2) in mauve straw

3) in purple velvet

4) in same pink + white check— but this model is too small for me

5) Soft suede beret to match enclosed blue linen sample

6) Black satin pillbox without the jet bangles— (the combs show when I put this on— should it be a little bigger or what?)

7) Pink velvet beret to match tiny sample of wool My secretary sent you, just

2) like the red suede one I ordered but without little point that sticks up—

Just send them all to 3307 N St so I'll have them by Jan 20— though I would like the black felt + pink velvet beret before—

For spring I will also need a navy blue hat to wear with Navy + white plaid coat— or perhaps white bound with Navy— it is a big white coat with navy blue blanket plaid lines on it.

Remember I like berets + souwesters for spring— in straw— the kind Dior used to have.

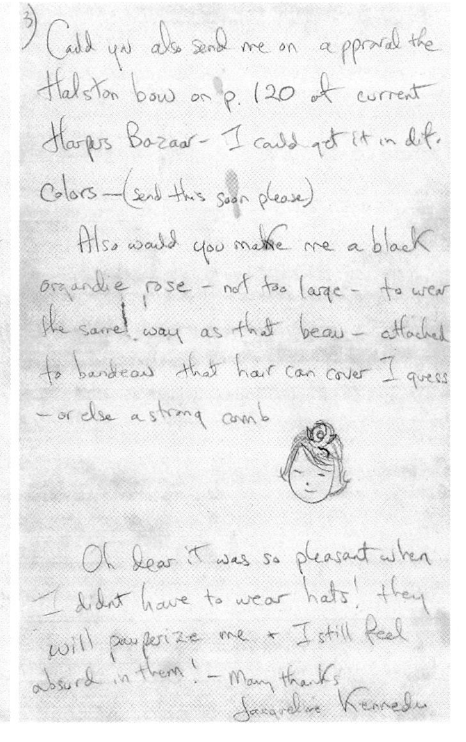
3) Could you also send me on approval the Halston bow on p. 120 of current Harpers Bazaar— I could get it in dif. colors—(send this soon please)

Also would you make me a black organdie rose— not too large— to wear the same way as that beau— attached to bandeau that hair can cover I guess— or else a strong comb

Oh dear it was so pleasant when I didnt have to wear hats! they will pauperize me + I still feel absurd in them!— Many thanks
Jacqueline Kennedy

designers—Galanos, Scaasi, and Norell among them—"are all too extreme," but that perhaps their clothes might work for her "in less wild materials." In the understated, costly clothes of Mainbocher, the American couturier who had defined the duchess of Windsor's image in the thirties, Mrs. Kennedy regretted that "I just look like a sad mouse." However, she conceded that he would be the best choice for her inaugural ball gown, "which it is really jumping the gun to think about." She added that it should be "in perfect taste—so simple & so beautiful."

Her letter to Mrs. Vreeland further stated, "I rather favor firms who make French copies—if they aren't too much known to be French." Mrs. Vreeland responded by suggesting an intriguing triumvirate of designers: Stella Sloat, Ben Zuckerman, and Norman Norell. Sloat defined the signature simplicity of her well-made sportswear separates as "what is left after you take everything away." Despite the thoroughly American feeling of her clothes, at times she included copies of Givenchy originals in her line. Romanian-born Ben Zuckerman was a fashion industry stalwart, working with his designer, Henry Shacter, to produce "the only clothes made in America that look as though Dior or Balenciaga made them." It was Zuckerman's line-for-line copy of a Pierre Cardin coat in purple wool that Jacqueline Kennedy had at first decided to wear for the inauguration-day ceremonies (she wore it instead to tour the White House with Mamie Eisenhower on December 9, 1960).

"It was natural the First Lady should go to America's First Designer," John Fairchild observed of her early choice of Norell, who had declared "I don't like over-designed anything." He drew inspiration from Jacqueline Kennedy's preferred couturiers, Chanel, Balenciaga, and Givenchy, and, as first lady, she continued to wear some of the understated day clothes that he made for her during this period.

As a gesture of thanks to Diana Vreeland, Jacqueline Kennedy chose to be photographed with the president-elect and their children by *Harper's Bazaar*'s Richard Avedon for the magazine's February 1961 issue (the cover of this publication was one of the images). On February 1 *Vogue*'s editor in chief, Jessica Daves, fired off a peevish letter to the White House press officer, Pierre Salinger, reminding him of the proposed sitting with Cecil Beaton, planned for October 1960, that Jacqueline Kennedy had postponed until after the inauguration. The Beaton sitting did not materialize, and the resoundingly elegant Avedon images would be the last formal photographs for which she would sit as first lady; she was determined to guard her young family's privacy in the face of relentless media interest. "My press relations will be minimum information given with maximum politeness" was the directive given to twenty-three-year-old Pamela Turnure, the first press secretary appointed to a first lady.

In addition to Mrs. Vreeland's choices, the designer Oleg Cassini, a Kennedy family friend, proposed himself as a candidate to work with the first lady, apparently at the suggestion of his brother Igor, the influential Hearst gossip columnist who had once named Jacqueline Bouvier "debutante of the year." Before the November 8 election Oleg Cassini wrote to Mrs.Kennedy with the assurance that "naturally, the dresses you would get here will be specially made

Opposite: Jacqueline Kennedy's letter of November 14, 1960, to Marita O'Connor, her millinery saleswoman at Bergdorf Goodman. This page, top: Halston, photographed with the actress Virna Lisi, 1964; at right, Kenneth Battelle's Billy Baldwin–decorated salon, illustrated by Henry Kohler for *Vogue*, 1963; bottom: Diana Vreeland, painted by René Bouché, ca.1960

for you, with your counsel and direction and in keeping with your marvelous sense of personal fashion."

In reply Jacqueline Kennedy asked Cassini to "get started designing me something, then send me some sketches and, if I like them, I can give you credit for doing most of my Spring wardrobe." The letter also reveals her intention, as first lady, to stay true to her established style. She asks for ideas for "some pretty, long evening dresses suitable for big official dinners. You know the kind I like: Balenciaga covered-up look. Even though these clothes are for official life, please don't make them dressy as I'm sure I can continue to dress the way I like—simple and young clothes, as long as they are covered up for the occasion."

The urbane Cassini, born in Paris to Russian parents and raised in Florence, became an American citizen in 1942. He had known Joseph P. Kennedy since the war. As Cassini remembers, it was Ambassador Kennedy who encouraged him to leave the Hollywood studio system (where he gained a reputation at Paramount with dramatic costumes for his wife Gene Tierney's starring vehicles *The Razor's Edge* and *Shanghai Gesture*) and to establish his own Seventh Avenue fashion house, which he did in 1950. In mid-December 1960 Jacqueline Kennedy decided to have Cassini coordinate her wardrobe. Joseph Kennedy instructed Cassini to send the bills to his office. "With great foresight," the designer noted, "he wanted to wipe out any possibility that the First Lady's new wardrobe might be used against them politically."

Mrs. Kennedy had already asked Bergdorf Goodman to work with her on designs for her inaugural ball gown. At one point, as she confided to Marita O'Connor, she had even considered entrusting Bergdorf's with the majority of her wardrobe. This would have been an effective conduit to the Paris designs that they reproduced with such skill. Bergdorf's continued with the inaugural ball gown (partly inspired by a dress by London designer Victor Stiebel), while Cassini undertook the dress for the inaugural gala. "Now I know how poor Jack feels when he has told 3 people they can be Secy. of State," she wrote Cassini on December 13, 1960, in a letter that spelled out her expectations. "Are you sure you are up to it, Oleg? Please say yes—there is so much detail about one's wardrobe once one is in the public eye. . . . I am counting on you to be a superb Wardrobe Mistress—every glove, shoe, hat, etc. & all delivered on time." Under the heading PUBLICITY she counseled discretion, adding "I know that I am so much more of fashion interest than other First Ladies—I refuse to have Jack's administration plagued by fashion stories of a sensational nature—& to be the Marie-Antoinette or Joséphine of the 1960s."

Through Letitia Baldrige Jacqueline Kennedy issued a statement (sent to *Women's Wear Daily* and women's-page editors on January 13) saying that she was "distressed by implications of extravagance, of over-emphasis of fashion in relation to her life, and of the misuse of her name by firms from which she has not bought clothes." Henceforth, *WWD* adopted a more respectful tone, dubbing the first lady "Her Elegance" and documenting almost every nuance of her fashion choices in scrupulous—and almost daily—detail. It was news when Mrs. Kennedy abandoned her characteristic triple strand of artificial pearls in favor of Chanel's long ropes. When she wore the same designer's ivory wool coat (p. 77), the newspaper stated, "It's the fashion today for the elite, but it's the Skinny Look for the masses . . . soon—if Her Elegance wears it." Mrs. Kennedy stayed gracefully above the fray. "Jackie had been criticized for wearing Paris dresses," noted Cecil Beaton, observing the first lady at an informal London dinner, "but she just laughed and seemed to have no fear of criticism. She enjoys so many aspects of the job, and takes for granted the more onerous onslaughts of the Press."

Mrs. Kennedy's choice of Oleg Cassini was greeted with some skepticism in the fashion world. "Everyone was surprised," wrote John Fairchild in *The Fashionable Savages* (1965). "He was debonair, amusing, social, but none of the fashion intellectuals had considered him an important designer." Cassini's provocatively formfitting, glamorous clothes owed more to his background as a Hollywood designer than to the Paris-inspired output of Seventh Avenue. His fashion shows had a nightclub ambience, with the designer himself addressing the audience with an often risqué comic monologue. "I like the alluring way women look in clothes that accentuate their femininity," he told one magazine. "I firmly believe it is an offense against nature to flatten, rather than flatter, their provocative curves. When I design a dress, I visualize a stunning girl wearing it on a date with me, and I don't want her to be mistaken for a prison matron. In my book, elegance and good taste do not require the total elimination of sex appeal." Cassini's clients included such Hollywood stars as Joan Crawford, Joan Fontaine, and Janet Leigh, who responded to his high-voltage effects.

Until his association with Jacqueline Kennedy, Cassini had remained one of the rare Seventh Avenue designers to declare independence from the hegemony of Paris couture, and he had lampooned Parisian innovations like the unfitted chemise dress. Cassini acknowledged that "I had to readjust my concept to fit the image of the first lady. I put a little water in my wine." He told *Women's Wear Daily* in 1964 that his "regular collection—which reflected my own personal attitudes—didn't represent what I did for Mrs. Kennedy. . . . I was trained to dress The Individual . . . in doing clothes for some 26 motion pictures. I learned that the story dictates the fashion. The Kennedy Story was an extremely elegant one and you could not experiment."

Cassini and his workrooms were solicitous of the requirements of a client with a powerful sense of her own identity. As Cassini noted, "I proposed and she disposed." In a syndicated newspaper article, "Mrs. Kennedy Revives Elegance," Cassini (as told to Stanley Frank) said of the first lady that "her taste is so impeccable that my job is essentially a matter of presenting ideas for her editing. Long before she moved into the White House and the public eye she knew the secret of true elegance is the art of eliminating every superfluous detail and accessory that distracts attention from a woman's personality." Cassini approached each project with a movie costume designer's eye, "envisioning how she would look in close ups or from a distance." He took Jacqueline Kennedy's references as starting points, simplifying and then exaggerating lines and details.

"Oleg was very cooperative," remembers Lee Radziwill, who worked with Cassini on some of her own clothes when she accompanied her sister to India and Pakistan. "He was never a prima donna. He genuinely wanted to please and make her life easier, and not make her life more complex by being offended or allowing clothes to take more of a place of importance than necessary in her life. And I think she really appreciated that; it was a very important reason for wanting to work with Oleg."

As she had done with her dressmaker Mini Rhea, and with Marita O'Connor and Ethel Frankau at Bergdorf Goodman, Jacqueline Kennedy sent the Cassini workrooms pages from fashion magazines such as *L'Officiel* and *Harper's Bazaar,* often with her own annotations or sketches suggesting adaptations. "I don't design my own clothes," Jacqueline Kennedy told the Boston *Globe* on August 30, 1960, "but I do choose becoming features from the different dresses I see. My dressmaker combines them into something for me." This interest began as a schoolgirl, when, as her close friend Nancy Tuckerman (who became

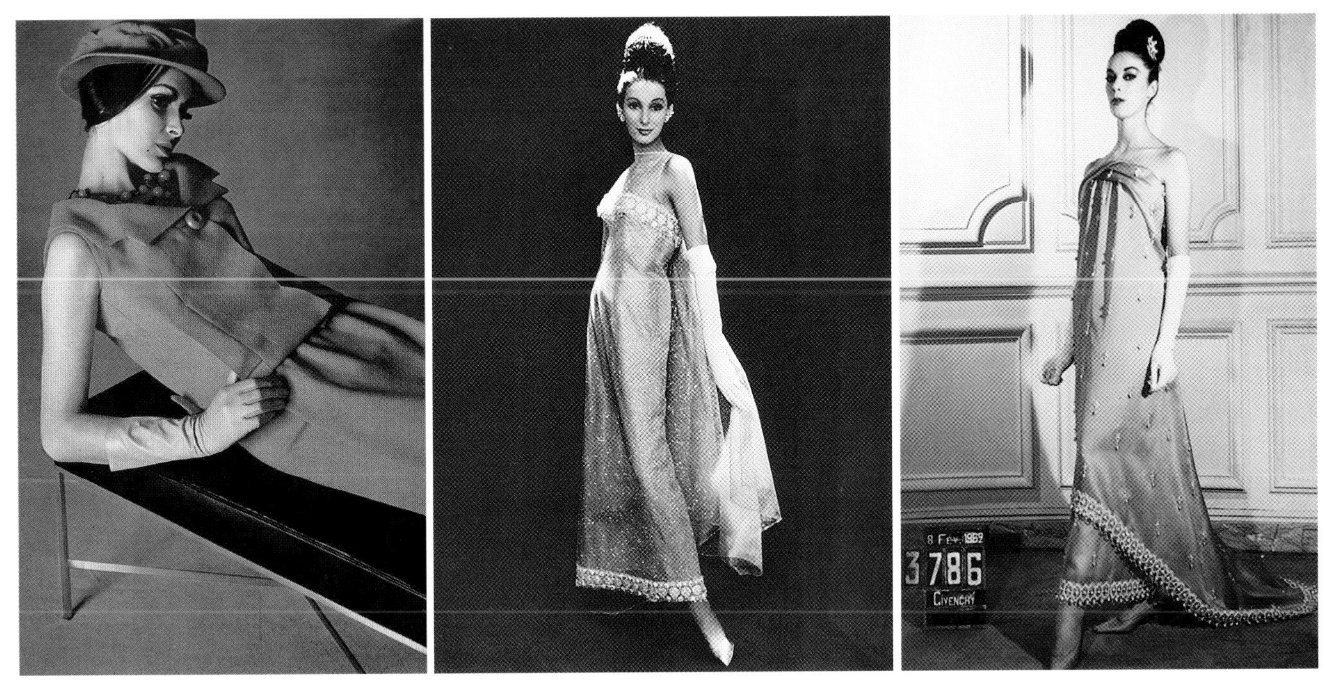

Opposite: Oleg Cassini presenting his designs for the film *The Razor's Edge* to director Edmund Goulding, photographed by Ralph Crane, 1946. This page: Inspirations, left to right: Karl Lagerfeld's suit for Jean Patou, photographed by Pottier for *L'Officiel de la Couture* (March 1962), which inspired the pink suit worn on the trip to Mexico (see p. 165); a Lagerfeld dress in the same issue, on which the dress Jacqueline Kennedy wore to a dinner honoring the president of the Ivory Coast was based (see p. 100); Hubert de Givenchy's spring–summer 1962 model number 3786

the first lady's social secretary in June 1963) remembers, Jacqueline Bouvier finished her test papers ahead of the rest of the class and then filled the time sketching her ideas for dresses on the backs of them.

"There wasn't a magazine printed that she didn't read and see!" remembers Kay McGowan, Cassini's showroom director. "She'd tear things out of magazines—ask for a higher neck or whatever." This was something she often did while Kenneth arranged her hair. "She was very heavy on Givenchy," he recalls. The first lady often specified the material that she wanted for her clothes, occasionally including swatches and even a length of fabric, usually from European fabric houses suggested to the first lady and Cassini by Diana Vreeland's office.

At times she submitted tracings of sketches from the Paris couture houses that her sister or stylish friends such as Jayne Wrightsman sent to her or that her office would solicit from the establishments themselves. (On January 2, 1962, for instance, Letitia Baldrige wrote to Letizia Mowinckel, "JBK is dying to know what Philippe Venet's collection of suits and coats looks like. He was Givenchy's tailor and evidently this is his first collection. If you can get a hold of any sketches for your 'cousin' plus prices, she would be thrilled.") Jacqueline Kennedy also sent original Paris couture clothing—items already in her wardrobe, borrowed from her sister, or obtained through Saks (where she acquired some of her Chanel and Givenchy originals)—to serve as starting points for an element of design or, in some instances, to be copied line-for-line in different fabrics.

Although Jacqueline Kennedy and Cassini discussed ideas together, he maintained a distance from the mechanics of producing her clothes, cherishing instead his position as a family friend. The efficient Kay McGowan, therefore, was put in charge of coordinating the first lady's clothing and accessories. She transmitted the ideas of Cassini, his design coordinator, Joseph Boccheir, and the first lady to the two workrooms. McGowan also served as liaison with the millinery department of Bergdorf Goodman, with the shoemaker Mr. Mario of Eugenia of Florence, and, initially, with Koret for evening bags (like the evening shoes, these were matched to the dresses). After General de Gaulle presented Mrs. Kennedy with a golden mesh minaudière from Van Cleef and Arpels, this became her ubiquitous—and influential—evening accessory.

Jacqueline Kennedy expressed her thanks in a letter to Kay McGowan. "Please tell Oleg I think we have done the most marvelous work together—it isn't just copying—but my ideas for what I need—plus his + your excellent workmen—We work together better than Gloria Guinness and Balenciaga ever did."

For the increasing demands of her state wardrobe, Jacqueline Kennedy did not require the subtleties of construction and detailing (often apparent only to the wearer) that the workrooms of the Paris couture provided. Instead, for gala entertaining as well as for her travel needs, her clothes above all had to be photogenic and easy to read in a crowd. Recalling the first lady's appearance at a Benares silk market on her India trip, for instance, Ambassador John Kenneth Galbraith

wrote that "with her excellent sense of theatre [she] had put on a lavender dress which could be picked out at any range up to five miles."

For Cassini, the collaboration with Mrs. Kennedy in developing her increasingly iconic style secured his own position in twentieth-century design. By October 1961 Eugenia Sheppard was reporting that "according to Tobé's most recent coast to coast survey, the best known name in American fashion is now Oleg Cassini."

As first lady Jacqueline Kennedy maintained a connection to the fashion world through stylish friends and through Lee Radziwill, who, living in London with her husband, Prince Stanislas, at the time, was well placed for forays to explore the Paris couture on her sister's behalf. "I'd tell her what I was very enthusiastic about," she remembers, "and if I thought something might be very useful for her. I think that was very helpful, because she couldn't concentrate on it as a full-time job. Of course I'd say what I thought was really pretty or get sketches and samples to send."

Diana Vreeland continued to bring to the first lady's attention fashion ideas and designers, including Guy Douvier, at Christian Dior–New York, and Gustave Tassell, a West Coast protégé of James Galanos. Mrs. Vreeland also coordinated designs with Emilio Pucci, whose bravura sports clothes the first lady chose for a holiday in Italy. For her private wardrobe Jacqueline Kennedy also wore the luxuriously casual clothes of Princess Irene Galitzine, a Roman couturiere who made a name for herself as the creator of "palazzo pyjamas."

Jacqueline Kennedy also experimented with fashionable resources of the moment, such as the Manhattan boutique A La Carte. It was run by Joan Morse, who later became a Warhol acolyte and who endearingly admitted "I can't sew, drape or cut a pattern. But I play with a piece of fabric and it comes up wild and it sells." At the opposite end of the spectrum was Chez Ninon, a couture salon established by socially well connected Nona Park and Sophie Shonnard in the late 1920s. "They were two wonderful, pixilated ladies," remembers Babs Simpson, a *Vogue* fashion editor at the time. "They'd go to Paris and terrorize everybody even though they had the tiniest shop!" Through Chez Ninon Jacqueline Kennedy acquired clothing that was legitimately made in America, although designed in Paris. Chez Ninon also employed in-house designers, who created their own models and adapted Paris couture originals for their socially distinguished clients.

Nicole Alphand, wife of the French ambassador to Washington during the Kennedy administration, was another influence in matters of taste and a conduit for news of French couture. At one time a Dior mannequin, Alphand was the paradigmatic ambassador's wife. Mme Alphand did much to promote French couture and its related arts in Washington and would eventually return to the fashion world as the director of Pierre Cardin's house.

Both Nicole Alphand and Lee Radziwill were involved in the elaborate sartorial preparations for Jacqueline Kennedy's tour of Europe in June 1961, which proved the defining moment for the first lady on the world stage. Radziwill helped select and adapt a model from Givenchy's collection for her sister to wear to Versailles, and Alphand was a liaison with Alexandre, the most celebrated hairdresser of his day. Alexandre recalls telling Mrs. Kennedy, "Madame, you are going chez Louis Quatorze, I will dress you like a queen!"

Opposite, top: Diana Vreeland and Lee Radziwill at a Christian Dior–New York fashion show, photographed by Eduardo E. Latour, February 1962; at right, the dress they selected from it for Mrs. Kennedy; bottom: Jacqueline Kennedy in Italy, August 1962. This page, top: Chez Ninon copied both "Passeport" (top right), by Marc Bohan for Christian Dior, and Givenchy's spring-summer 1961 model number 3270 for the first lady; bottom: Lee Radziwill in Givenchy, photographed by Henry Clarke for *Vogue,* 1960

In France the Givenchy clothes that Jacqueline Kennedy chose to augment her Cassini wardrobe were seen as a gesture of respect to the host nation. The painstaking image that she cultivated had a resounding impact on fashion as well as in political terms. As the first lady's stepbrother Yusha Auchincloss observed, she set off for Paris "with the thought of her husband and de Gaulle as sort of a continuation of the historic association between George Washington and General Lafayette."

Ambassador Hervé Alphand noted, "I think her influence was extremely efficient as far as Franco-American relations were concerned. . . . Jacqueline helped [President Kennedy] very much to understand France." And Pearl Buck wrote, "It was a source of pride to me that she appeared in France simply but well dressed and that she spoke to the French people in their own tongue."

Jacqueline Kennedy's appeal in France was such that the following year she made a goodwill tour to India and Pakistan, this time without the president. "This is Mrs. Kennedy's first semiofficial trip by herself," Pamela Turnure announced on the eve of her departure. "She feels, and hopes, that it will be more memorable than just a group of fashion stories." This was a vain hope. Again, Jacqueline Kennedy's wardrobe was assembled with an eye for effective juxtapositions and dramatic effects. As with the wardrobe for all her trips, this, too, had a significant influence on the fashion industry. "Buyers are counting on a boom in everything Indian when the First Lady returns," wrote *WWD*.

From the shocking pink Cassini coat that she wore on her arrival in India to the shining yellow Tassell dress that she chose for an elephant ride, Mrs. Kennedy's every outfit was a dazzling photo opportunity and helped to reinforce the positive world view of America. Ambassador Galbraith, in a telegram to the president, humorously lamented: "Plan to soft pedal on clothes rivalling success of Stassen's efforts to ditch Nixon. Now they are asking who designed mine." "Despite her best efforts," wrote *Life*'s Anne Chamberlain, "her every seam has been the subject of hypnotized attention from the streets of Delhi to the Khyber Pass."

Although Jacqueline Kennedy's overseas tours were culturally oriented, they also served a deeper political purpose. The cold war was raging, and the Kennedy administration was wary, for instance, of Soviet interest in India and especially in Latin America, where President Kennedy sought to improve relations through his Alliance for Progress initiative. When she accompanied her husband on these trips, the first lady once more proved a powerful and potent asset, and, as the president noted, her presence was insurance of a big crowd and safe treatment.

At home Jacqueline Kennedy taught the nation the transformative possibilities of beauty, culture, and artistic expression and conveyed her profound belief in the resonance of history in contemporary life. When, as *Life*'s Hugh Sidey wrote, she "showed the world that there was unimagined strength beneath the silk," she taught the country that style was a state of being, and, in so doing, she allowed the national spirit to soar once more.

This page: Nicole Alphand, dressed by Nina Ricci and photographed by Michael A. Vaccaro for *Look,* April 26, 1960; right: Givenchy's sketch and Hurel's embroidery for Mrs. Kennedy's Versailles dress, 1961. Opposite: Mrs. Kennedy and Lee Radziwill on Lake Pichola, India, March 17,1962

Campaign

Although he did not officially announce his presidential candidacy until January 1960, John F. Kennedy set out to establish a stronger national profile in the fall of 1959. As Jacques Lowe, one of the photographers who accompanied Kennedy on most of his campaign odyssey, remembered in his *Portrait: The Emergence of John F. Kennedy* (1961), "There are few lonelier ordeals than the pre-primary campaign of a Presidential hopeful. . . . but he was comforted in those days by the almost constant presence of his wife. She presided at teas in Oregon and at farm-equipment auctions in the Midwest." Jacqueline Kennedy's compelling charm and ability to connect with people, together with her linguistic skills—famously proficient in French and Spanish, she also acquired some Polish and Italian on the trail—made her a valuable asset in this formative period of her husband's run for the presidency.

By mid-1960 she had become a cynosure of press interest. *Life* magazine, covering the campaign in Wisconsin, noted that "the candidate's striking wife Jackie, who sticks close to her husband, has attracted almost as much attention as he has. Women crane to see what she is wearing. Voters of both sexes bombard her with questions, many of them curiously unpolitical . . . the kind of questions usually put to a Hollywood movie queen." That July, the month her husband accepted the Democratic nomination for president, *Time* characterized her in rapturous fashion as "a limpid beauty who would have excited Goya into mixing his rose madder. Jackie is the quintessence of cultured, luminous womanhood. . . . she has made her own determined amendments to the tribal laws, restricting her campaigning to such niceties as wowing the Louisiana Cajuns with a speech in Sorbonne French, and entertaining politicians at her Georgetown home with fine food, vintage wine and sparkling conversation. . . . If her husband reaches the White House, Jackie will be the most exquisite First Lady since Frances Cleveland."

The beauteous Frances Folsom, who had married President Grover Cleveland in 1886, during his first term of office, had been celebrated for invigorating the White House and for her forward-thinking tastes in fashion. She was popularly credited with bringing about the demise of the bustle—a contraption she abhorred. Although during the campaign, as Lowe reveals, Jacqueline Kennedy, too, rejected some of the elaborateness of conventional female attire, "reducing her wardrobe to three basic dresses, a string of pearls and a hat," the Francophile distinction of her personal style drew some unwelcome media attention. The gossipy fashion-trade paper *Women's Wear Daily* published the supposed couture expenditures of Jacqueline Kennedy and her mother-in-law, Rose Kennedy, and this report was picked up and sensationalized by the national press. Pat Nixon, the wife of John Kennedy's opponent (Richard Nixon, the sitting vice president), responded with a stirring defense of American designers. The momentum created by this stage-managed contretemps would later result in the first lady's entrusting a U.S.-based designer, Oleg Cassini, with coordinating her "official" wardrobe.

In the meantime Jacqueline Kennedy's style was something of a bulwark against the arduous grind of the campaign trail. "Not many people know how physically wearing such a campaign can be," she was to recall. "Some mornings you're up at seven, and you visit a dozen towns during the day. You shake hundreds of hands in the afternoon and hundreds more at night. You get so tired you catch yourself laughing and crying at the same time. But you pace yourself and you get through it. You just look at it as something you have to do. You knew it would come and you knew it was worth it."

Finally, in the advanced stages of pregnancy, Jacqueline Kennedy, then thirty, retired from the campaign. She continued to contribute from the sidelines, as with her nationally syndicated "Campaign Wife" column, which served as a response to the increasing weight of her public mail. In one of these articles she pointedly addressed the furor over her personal taste. "All the talk over what I wear and how I fix my hair has amused and puzzled me," she wrote. "What does my hairdo have to do with my husband's ability to be President?"

French (designer unknown). Knit suit in asparagus green wool jersey with ivory linen trim, ca. 1959. Jacques Lowe photographic sitting, Georgetown, Washington, D.C., spring 1959. □ This French suit (probably from the boutique of a Paris couturier) reflects Jacqueline Kennedy's preference for unfitted clothing. Subtle details of workmanship belie the sportif aspect of the blouson jacket—the canted "ribbon" trim has been cut luxuriously from a single piece of fabric, for instance, and the crisply starched organdy collar attaches to the neckline by means of a series of press studs, so that it is detachable for hand laundering.

French (designer unknown). Tunic dress and skirt in ivory raw-silk shantung, ca. 1959. Mark Shaw photographic session for *Life* magazine, Georgetown, Washington, D.C., 1959. Visit to El Jardín de Infancia Don Simón kindergarten in Caracas, Venezuela, December 16, 1961. □ By the late fifties adventuresome Paris couturiers were moving away from the elaborate construction that had characterized their work since the war. This innovative tunic dress, evidently the product of a French couture house (and related to examples by both Grès and Givenchy), relies for its shape not on seaming but on the crisp body of its fabric, on gathering, and on the form within. Its geometric cut is emphasized by the topstitching details. □ Despite *Women's Wear Daily*'s characterization of the presidential candidate's chic wife as something of a haute couture spendthrift, Jacqueline Kennedy took a careful approach to the establishment of her wardrobe. A muslin tag sewn inside the hem of the tunic indicates that this ensemble was probably from the designer's runway showroom collection. Such garments were generally disposed of *en solde* (at greatly discounted prices) at the end of the season, a privilege usually extended to friends of the fashion houses who have model-sized figures. As Jacqueline Kennedy filled these criteria (Rose Kennedy had been a faithful Paris couture client since the late 1920s and also bought clothes for her daughter-in-law) and preferred clothing that was neither too emphatically of the moment nor precisely fitted to her form, such sales were a useful and economical way for her to acquire couture-quality clothes. She also bought clothes in this manner from the custom departments of New York stores. Even in the White House, she would continue to acquire some Paris items for her private life in this way. □ Jacqueline Kennedy wore this ensemble for a 1959 photographic session with Mark Shaw (in which he documented her rounds as a conscientious Georgetown hostess, ostensibly shopping for flowers, groceries, and books) for a *Life* magazine article entitled "Jackie: A Front Runner's Appealing Wife," which appeared in the August 24, 1959, issue. The timeless lines of this ensemble allowed her to keep it in her wardrobe, and she wore it two years later during the Kennedys' state visit to Venezuela.

Hubert de Givenchy (French, born 1927). Dress in fuschia silk shantung with ruffle, spring–summer 1958. Model number 2218. Jacques Lowe photographic sitting, Hyannis Port, Massachusetts, 1959. □ Cristobal Balenciaga's preferred dressmaking technique was to fit an underdress exactly to the body and then make the garment itself a little larger, the air current between the layers allowing movement and merely suggesting the forms beneath; the overblouse dress is an example of this technique. Here, Givenchy exaggerated the principle and the unfitted line that Jacqueline Kennedy endorsed, creating a dress with a structure all its own that becomes a carapace standing away from the figure. □ She wore this dress in Hyannis Port for a Jacques Lowe photographic sitting with her husband and Caroline; a family portrait from this session would become the Kennedys' Christmas card later that year. Lowe, originally hired by *Collier's* to photograph Robert F. Kennedy, eventually joined the presidential campaign as a photographer.

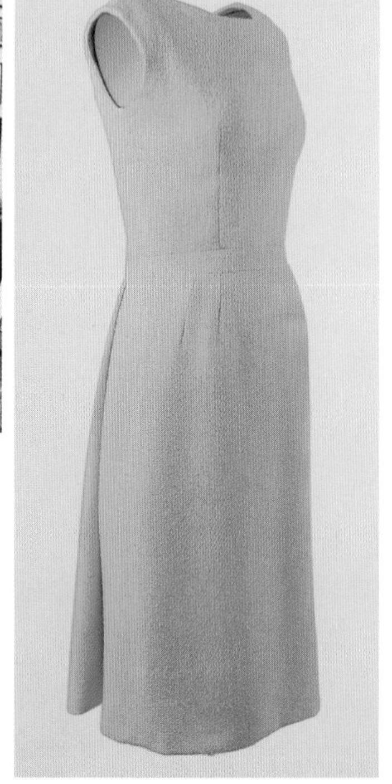

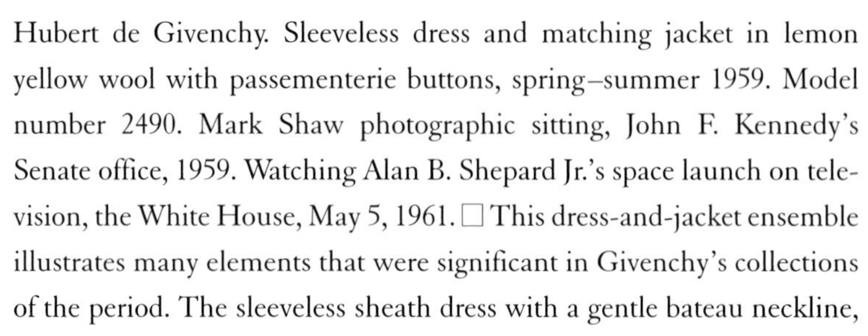

Hubert de Givenchy. Sleeveless dress and matching jacket in lemon yellow wool with passementerie buttons, spring–summer 1959. Model number 2490. Mark Shaw photographic sitting, John F. Kennedy's Senate office, 1959. Watching Alan B. Shepard Jr.'s space launch on television, the White House, May 5, 1961. □ This dress-and-jacket ensemble illustrates many elements that were significant in Givenchy's collections of the period. The sleeveless sheath dress with a gentle bateau neckline, worn with or without a boxy jacket, and the jacket's three-quarter-length sleeves and standaway collar (a Balenciaga innovation designed to isolate and attenuate the neck) are details that would remain leitmotifs in Jacqueline Kennedy's wardrobe as first lady. The lessons in fashion geometry that Givenchy absorbed from Balenciaga, his mentor, are here expressed in the triangular equilibrium of button placement; the single button at the neck of the jacket is balanced by the two that define the suggestion of vents in the back. □ Mark Shaw photographed Jacqueline Kennedy wearing this ensemble in her husband's senatorial office. With an adjustment of skirt length, she kept it in her White House wardrobe and wore it when she joined her husband, Vice President Lyndon B. Johnson, Special Assistant Arthur M. Schlesinger Jr., and other members of the White House staff in the office of the president's personal secretary, Evelyn Lincoln, where Jacques Lowe photographed them watching astronaut Alan Shepard's historic suborbital flight on May 5, 1961. (Three weeks earlier Russian cosmonaut Yuri Gagarin had been the first to travel beyond the earth's atmosphere.) Later that same month President Kennedy urged Congress to set a national goal of sending a man to the moon and returning him safely before the end of the decade.

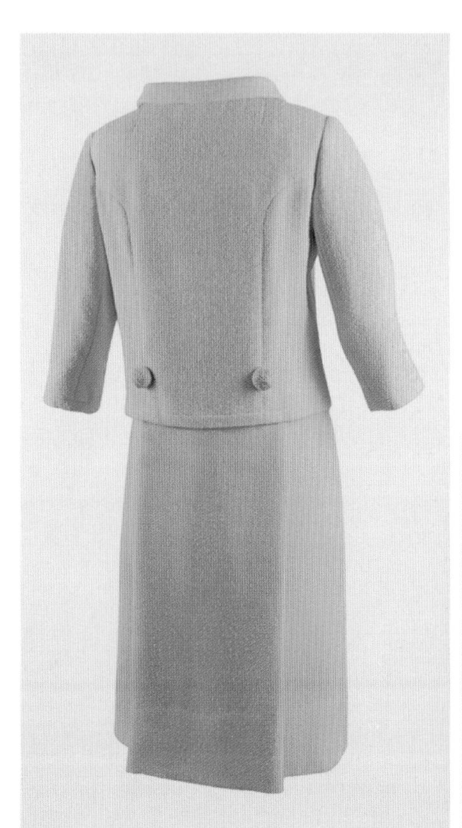

Bob Bugnand (French, born 1924). Suit in black-and-white–houndstooth wool tweed with black braided trim, ca. 1959. Presidential campaign, fall 1959–spring 1960. □ Like Christian Dior and Hubert de Givenchy before him, Bob Bugnand trained with the Parisian couturiers Lelong and Piguet, each celebrated for his flattering, client-friendly clothes. After this blue-chip apprenticeship Bugnand opened his own salon in Paris before establishing a branch in New York in 1957. Although his fashionable clients (among them Babe Paley, the stylish wife of CBS chairman William Paley, their daughter Amanda Mortimer, and Judy Peabody) were fitted in New York, their clothes were made in Bugnand's Paris workrooms, thus providing, as noted by *Harper's Bazaar,* "French workmanship without the necessity of a passport"—an indication of the cachet of Paris couture. A 1958 review by Eugenia Sheppard, the influential women's-page editor of the New York *Herald Tribune,* noting that "a steady stream of chic young women had flocked to his salon," brought Bugnand to the attention of Jacqueline Kennedy. The designer's understated aesthetic and Parisian credentials appealed to her. Here, Bugnand abstracted the notion of Chanel's influential postwar suit (with its sloping-shouldered cardigan jacket edged in braided trim, skirt cut with a gentle ease of movement, and textural tweed check) to provide an outfit of graphic but subdued elegance.

Campaign

Hubert de Givenchy, for Givenchy Boutique (French, established 1952). Dress and overblouse in slate gray wool jersey, ca. 1959. Presidential campaign, fall 1959–spring 1960. □ With Jacqueline Kennedy's endorsement, the overblouse dress was a Parisian innovation that was adopted into America's popular fashion vocabulary. This wool jersey example was made for the boutique that Givenchy had launched in 1952 at the same time that he opened his fashion house. During this period the boutique was a complement to the youthful spirit of his couture collection, but by the late 1950s, when his clothes reflected the authoritative distinction of his mentor, Balenciaga, the boutique's focus had shifted. Now, this collection—noted by *Vogue* as "known to fashion savants as a Way of Life"—adapted the lines of successful models from past seasons in less expensive textiles. Jacqueline Kennedy had little time or patience for fittings generally required for couture garments, so the boutique clothes, which required fewer or no fittings, were an ideal solution. □ Although this is not a haute-couture piece, the legerdemain of the Givenchy workrooms is nevertheless revealed in the sculptural molding of material as pliant as wool jersey. The overblouse, as deceptively simple as a sweater, has a neckline that was cut to stand up and away from the shoulder blades and a deep bias band at the hem that impedes its fall. Givenchy achieved layering without bulk by "shrugging" the overblouse over the dress's hidden, light silk top. These skillful contrivances created an effect of absolute simplicity—although the ensemble was admittedly distinguished enough to stand out in the refuge of an Oregon diner on the campaign trail. □ Above, the Kennedys share an impromptu moment with Vice President Richard M. Nixon.

JACK

Hubert de Givenchy. Coat in scarlet double-faced wool, fall–winter 1959. Model number 2680. Presidential campaign, fall 1959. Press conference announcing John F. Kennedy's candidacy for president, U.S. Capitol, Washington, D.C., January 2, 1960. □ During the campaign Eugenia Sheppard applauded Jacqueline Kennedy's Givenchy "anemone" coats in vivid red and purple. Following press criticism of Mrs. Kennedy's taste for expensive Parisian fashion, this one (dubbed the "good luck coat" by its owner) was "highly publicized as an Ohrbach's copy," noted *Women's Wear Daily* in an editorial published during election week, adding their contention that it was "actually . . . a Paris original." □ Ohrbach's, the popular New York department store, devised an inspired (and influential) marketing tool: it created line-for-line copies of couture clothes—often in their original fabrics—and presented them in tandem with the Parisian prototypes in glamorously attended fashion shows where, according to *Life* magazine, "women [fought] to buy them at prices as low as $40." At Ohrbach's Jacqueline Kennedy supplemented her French originals with inexpensive and effective interpretations. The workmanship and detailing of this particular garment, however, appear to support *WWD*'s contention. Givenchy transformed the double-faced coat, using the welted seams to describe a subtle, inverted goblet shape that curves from an Empire waist. □ Mrs. Kennedy wore this coat during the fall of 1959, here reading Jack Kerouac aboard the *Caroline,* the ten-seat plane, complete with small sleeping compartment, that the Kennedy family purchased to ease the grueling pace of the campaign.

Campaign

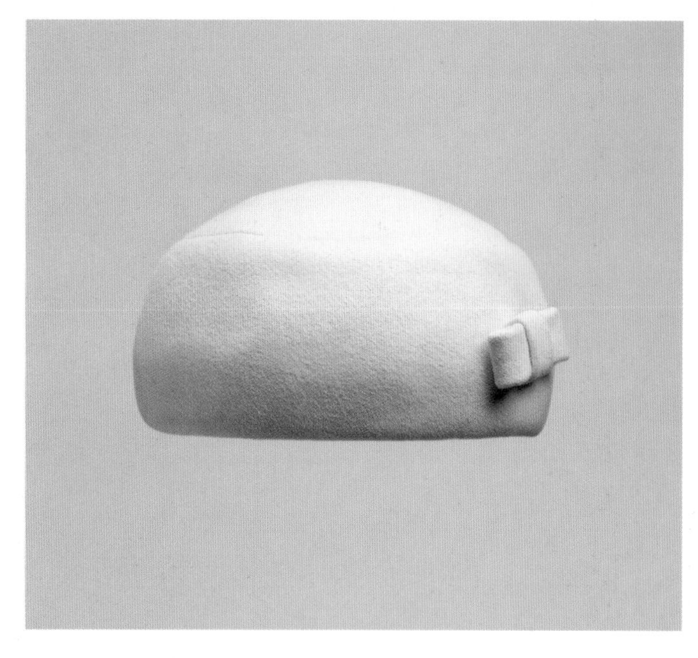

Hubert de Givenchy. Pillbox hat in white felt, ca. 1960. Ticker-tape parade, Times Square, New York City, October 19, 1960. □ A crowd of two million people thronged the streets of midtown Manhattan to see the presidential candidate and his glamorous wife in a triumphant ticker-tape parade three weeks before the election. Although it was late in her pregnancy, Jacqueline Kennedy continued to present a vision of controlled Francophile elegance, having chosen the felicitous volume of a wide-cut Givenchy coat, balanced with the designer's perverse (but essentially Parisian) diminution of the pillbox hat. She abhorred hats, but this form (that both Givenchy and Balenciaga had sponsored) complemented the volume of her hair, which had been arranged by Kenneth Battelle since the early 1950s, and it was a style that she would have reinterpreted frequently by the custom-hat department at Bergdorf Goodman.

KENNEDY
FOR PRESIDENT
LEADERSHIP FOR THE 60's

Inauguration

The inaugural festivities of January 19 and 20, 1961, set the tone of cultural enlightenment that the Kennedy administration, and Jacqueline Kennedy in particular, would continue to foster actively in the White House. Le Moyne Billings, a friend of John F. Kennedy's since preparatory school, recalled that the president-elect, who shared his wife's profound interest in history, "deliberately decided to invest his inauguration with pomp and ceremony. He wanted to use the moment to appeal to the imagination, to raise the ceremony to a heightened level of feeling." The historical resonance of this event was given physical expression by the Kennedys' considered sartorial statements.

General Eisenhower had worn a business suit and a homburg to his first inauguration in 1953; Kennedy, in a patrician cutaway and a silk top hat, preferred to stress his own continuity with tradition. Despite the biting cold, he discarded his overcoat to deliver the inaugural address, projecting an image of youthful vigor. Jacqueline Kennedy's fashion choices also set her apart from the crowd. These harbingers of her approach to state apparel would crystallize in the "Jackie look"—a dashing synthesis of begloved propriety, discreet historicism, and reductive modernity. For the inaugural gala on the nineteenth she wore a regal gown with train and symbolic cockade by Oleg Cassini. The program on that first evening began with a fanfare composed for the occasion and conducted by Leonard Bernstein; it also included a reading by Eleanor Roosevelt from Lincoln's writings and performances by Laurence Olivier, Fredric March, Mahalia Jackson, and Ella Fitzgerald, as well as by Frank Sinatra, who had organized the event. For the following evening's inaugural balls the first lady wore a dress and cape that she had designed herself in collaboration with the Bergdorf Goodman department store.

At the inauguration Jacqueline Kennedy appeared in Cassini's understated yet eminently photogenic greige (gray-beige) coat, with a domed pillbox hat from Bergdorf Goodman. The latter was to become an enduring symbol of her potent fashion impact. Before the swearing-in Marian Anderson sang "The Star-Spangled Banner" and, at Jacqueline Kennedy's instigation, eighty-six-year-old Robert Frost recited his poem "The Gift Outright." Frost, the country's unofficial poet laureate, had also written a new poem, which began by expressing his and other artists' pleasure at being welcomed so warmly at "august occasions of the state." ("Unlike most Americans," wrote the Boston *Globe*'s Kate Lang of the Kennedys, "they find poetry nourishing, rather than frightening.")

In his address the new president defined the spirit of his "New Frontier," declaring that "the torch has been passed to a new generation of Americans—born in this century, tempered by war, disciplined by a hard and bitter peace, proud of our ancient heritage," and he bid all citizens of the world to "ask not what America will do for you, but what together we can do for the freedom of man." Although Jacqueline Kennedy had heard the speech "in bits and pieces many times while he was working on it in Florida," she remembered that "when I heard it as a whole for the first time, it was so pure and beautiful and soaring that I knew I was hearing something great. And now I know that it will go down in history as one of the most moving speeches ever uttered—with Pericles' Funeral Oration and the Gettysburg Address."

NO
EXIT

Oleg Cassini (born in France, 1913). Evening gown in ivory double-faced silk satin twill, 1961. Inaugural gala, National Guard Armory, Washington, D.C., January 19, 1961. □ This majestic dress, so suggestive of a bride or a debutante, was a masterstroke of image making, establishing Jacqueline Kennedy in the national consciousness as a woman of commanding personal style, with an unerring sense of history and of her place in it. The dress relied for effect on the splendor of its fabric and the assured simplicity of its lines. In these respects it had the stately impact of a Balenciaga (in fact, it bears a resemblance to an inaccurate "preview" sketch, published by *Women's Wear Daily* on November 22, 1960, of Balenciaga's wedding gown for Doña Fabiola's marriage to King Baudouin of the Belgians, a dress also made in "tapestry thick" double-faced twill). □ The dress's color was symbolic; a letter to influential fashion editor Diana Vreeland reveals that Jacqueline Kennedy considered white "the most ceremonial color," and she chose shades of it for both her inaugural gown for Thursday's gala and her inaugural dress for Friday's balls. A contemporary newscaster noted that "the other Kennedy ladies got together and agreed they would eschew white as a color and leave it for the belle of the ball." Otherwise stripped of embellishment, the dress has a single telling detail in the cockade that hovers at the waist. It was an element that pointed to Jacqueline Kennedy's pride in her French Bouvier ancestry, her profound love of history, and her particular affinity with the eighteenth century. A formalized rosette of fabric, the cockade had its roots on the field of battle, where it was worn as a badge of loyalty, different colors indicating particular allegiances. During the American Revolution, for instance, Washington's soldiers wore black cockades. When Lafayette joined them, he adopted a black-and-white cockade to indicate his twin loyalties to America and Louis XVI, and the Continental army, as a gesture of respect to Lafayette, followed suit. □ An early press sketch from the Cassini studios reveals that the designer had originally considered placing this element high on the chest—a medal of honor, perhaps, or a winner's rosette. During fittings it slipped to the waist, where it focused attention instead on the break of the skirt. The illusion of a trained overskirt, opening to reveal the skirt beneath, had a decidely *dix-huitième* impact, an effect enhanced by the voluminous upswept hairstyle that Kenneth had contrived for Mrs. Kennedy. □ Thus attired, Jacqueline Kennedy stepped out into the snow with the president-elect for a concert at Constitution Hall, followed by the gala at the National Guard Armory. Kennedy's friend William Walton rode with them through the icy streets. Ever mindful of the crowds who had braved the blizzard, Kennedy asked Walton to "turn on the lights so they can see Jackie."

Inauguration

Oleg Cassini. Coat in greige wool melton, 1961. Sable muff, 1961. Inauguration ceremony, Washington, D.C., January 20, 1961. □ Late on the morning of January 20 the president-elect and Mrs. Kennedy left their eighteenth-century Georgetown house for the last time to make their way to the White House, where they joined the new vice president, the outgoing president and vice president, and their wives before driving on to the Capitol. □ Jacqueline Kennedy's ensemble for the ceremony defined the elegant simplicity and totality of visual image that would be the keynotes of her wardrobe as first lady. Every element was carefully considered; hat, coat, gloves, boots, and muff were orchestrated into a perfectly balanced whole. The surprising and atypical choice of a neutral greige color was a brilliant one, for in this pale, unemphatic, and unostentatious hue, Mrs. Kennedy stood out from all the other women swathed in deep, jewel-colored coats and dark furs, such as those worn by Mamie Eisenhower, Eunice Kennedy Shriver, and Lady Bird Johnson (below). The coat affirmed Oleg Cassini's graphic vision for Jacqueline Kennedy's state clothing. There is a suggestion of the Paris couture in its A-line swing and standaway neckline, but Cassini's background as a Hollywood costume designer is revealed in the emboldened detailing of the overscaled pockets and buttons ("a favorite fashion accent of mine," Cassini noted; "on Seventh Avenue, some would call me Mr. Button"). A sable circlet tucked into the collar echoed the muff. The new first lady set out for the White House wearing her classic unadorned pumps ("elegant and timeless," as she described them) but later braved the snow in fur-trimmed boots—another touch that has proved to be an enduring fashion influence. On this day she brought high style into the national arena. □ The sable muff, a discreet reference to the fur coats that many of the prominent women guests chose to wear on this glacial day, was the inspiration of Diana Vreeland. "It was only for practical reasons—I thought she was going to freeze to death," mused Vreeland in her autobiography, *D.V.* She qualified this statement with a sentiment that would have had far more resonance for both of them: "But I think muffs are so romantic because they have to do with *history*."

Oleg Cassini. Overblouse dress in beige wool crepe, 1961. Inauguration ceremony, Washington, D.C., January 20, 1961. □ For the luncheon at the Old Supreme Court Chamber that followed the swearing-in, the new first lady (shown here with Alabama Senator John J. Sparkman, cochairman of the Inaugural Committee) revealed a slender variant of the overblouse dress, designed by Oleg Cassini as a counterpoint to the A-line volume of the inaugural coat. Eschewing the unfitted silhouette traditionally associated with the overblouse dress, Cassini instead indulged his own preference for formfitting clothes and dressmaker details. Jacqueline Kennedy embellished the dress's controlled simplicity with a whimsical diamond-and-ruby berry-sprig clip, a gift from the president-elect to celebrate the birth of their son John F. Kennedy Jr. The brooch was the work of Jean Schlumberger, Tiffany's innovative master jeweler, who was characterized by *Vogue* as "a Renaissance goldsmith in the middle of the 20th century" and whose work, discovered and promoted by Elsa Schiaparelli in the 1930s, remained a favorite of the midcentury's preeminent women of style.

Bergdorf Goodman. Pillbox hat in beige felt, 1961. Inauguration ceremony, Washington, D.C., January 20, 1961. □ In the early fall of 1960 Jacqueline Kennedy, forced by her public role to embrace the formalized protocol of hat wearing, turned to Bergdorf Goodman's custom millinery salon, which specialized in reproducing Paris couture models and had for a year been fostering the talents of Roy Halston Frowick, whom Diana Vreeland considered "probably the greatest hatmaker in the world and an absolute magician with his hands." On December 19 Jacqueline Kennedy's office wrote to her saleswoman at Bergdorf's to suggest that what Mrs. Kennedy would consider "pretty for the Inauguration day parade" was "the big white felt hat" she had borrowed during the campaign. She had subsequently ordered this same shape in black leather and worn it on Election Day in Hyannis Port. "It should be in felt, the same color as the coat and stiff, not collapsible," the letter continued; a sample of the beige felt was included. With his fall–winter 1959 collection Givenchy had shown distinctively domed pillbox hats—pneumatic enlargements of the original pillbox or *tambourin* that had been, in various incarnations, a millinery staple since the 1930s—and it was a variant on this seamless, molded shape, reinterpreted by Halston, that Jacqueline Kennedy chose to complete her inauguration-day outfit. □ In their recent collections Givenchy, Saint Laurent at Dior, and Balenciaga had all shown similar hats worn straight and high on the head. Jacqueline Kennedy, however, "wanted her face to show, but she also didn't want her hair to get flattened out," noted her hairdresser, Kenneth Battelle. She was thus inspired to tip-tilt her hats to the back of her head. Ironically, this attempt to downplay the hat's scale and significance made instant fashion history and created an iconic element of style.

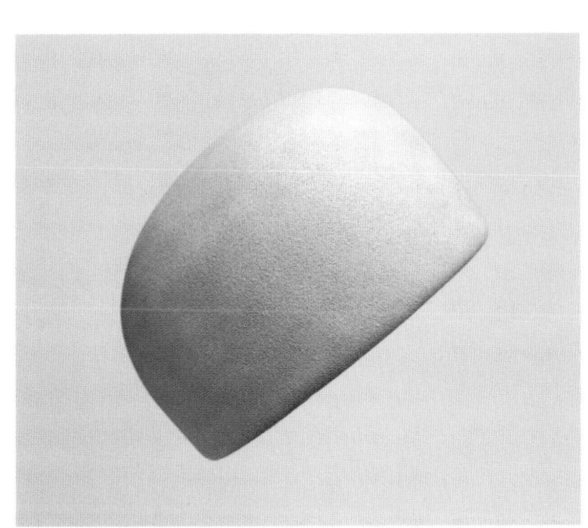

Bergdorf Goodman. Designed by Jacqueline Kennedy, with Emeric Partos (Hungarian, 1905–1975) and Ethel Frankau (American, 1880–1971). Cape in ivory silk faille and ivory silk georgette, 1961. Courtesy of the National Museum of American History. Inaugural balls, Washington, D.C., January 20, 1961. □ Jacqueline Kennedy worked in tandem with Diana Vreeland and Ethel Frankau, the distinguished fashion director of Bergdorf Goodman, on the design of her inaugural ball gown. An undated letter to Vreeland reveals her design methods: "Here is the picture [of a dress by Victor Stiebel] I tore out of some English magazine of what I think I would like the Inaugural Ball dress to be. . . . I imagine it is silver and white with a faille skirt. I also imagine the lines are the same as the enclosed Dior picture with the dark beaded top. I would like to modify the long bodice—so it doesn't look like a Dior of this season—something more timeless." Emeric Partos, Bergdorf's talented fur designer, unified the concept. Bergdorf Goodman's design sketch (above right) was published in *Vogue* on February 1, 1961. Although the elaborate embroidery of the bodice was appropriate to the stateliness of the occasion, Mrs. Kennedy characteristically downplayed it by veiling the bodice with a chiffon overblouse. This was caught at the hipline in an interpretation of the undefined-waist silhouette that Marc Bohan had shown in his recent debut collection for Dior. □ The cape, at once stately and romantic, was a late-in-the-day inspiration of Jacqueline Kennedy's, who at one point had considered a short fur jacket. Its luxurious interior finishing, such as the flourish of silk piping at the arm openings, reveals Bergdorf's exacting standards. As Bergdorf's did not have enough of the dress fabric to make the cape, nor anything that would be an exact match, the matte faille was veiled in chiffon georgette. The result diffused the solidity of the cape's form and created a shimmeringly ethereal effect. Stanley Woodward, chairman of the inaugural balls, recalled that Mrs. Kennedy "stopped everybody dead in their tracks."

Mrs. Kennedy

White House Style

Jacqueline Kennedy came to the White House determined to transform it into a theater of culture and taste. She was frankly appalled to discover the chief executive's mansion languishing in a state of aesthetic neglect and largely bereft of historically appropriate furnishings. As first lady, therefore, she lost no time in appointing the first White House curator and in forming the Fine Arts Committee for the White House, for which she enlisted socially prominent collectors and philanthropists. Together, they set to work to unearth period furnishings, paintings, and objects. "Everything in the White House must have a reason for being there," Jacqueline Kennedy told *Life*'s Hugh Sidey. "It would be sacrilege merely to redecorate it—a word I hate. It must be restored, and that has nothing to do with decoration. That is a question of scholarship."

Seeking a familiar setting for her young family—less a question of scholarship than of continuity and elegant comfort—Jacqueline Kennedy engaged Sister Parish, who had decorated the Kennedys' Georgetown house, to refurbish the private rooms on the second floor. It was the distinguished decorator Stéphane Boudin of the Paris firm Jansen, however, who presided over the state rooms below, drawing on the legacy of Thomas Jefferson and James Monroe for historical precedent. The result was a triumph of sophisticated Francophile elegance.

At the same time as Jacqueline Kennedy physically reinvented the White House as a museum of presidential history, she also departed from recently established patterns of presidential entertaining. State dinners were conceived with imagination and executed with bravura style. The first lady's fashions, food, flowers, music—even topics of conversation—were carefully orchestrated to project and reinforce the Kennedy image of vital intelligence, high culture, and youthful sophistication. Visiting dignitaries and other guests were treated to musicales (of which the Pablo Casals concert was the most celebrated) and performances by some of the country's preeminent dancers, singers, and actors. In January 1962, under the headline "BARDS AND BALLET DANCERS WHERE THE DIVOTS USED TO FLY," *Look* magazine commented that, "inspired by the New Frontier spirit, Washington is striving to erase a long-held notion—that, compared to other world capitals, it's a cultural hick town where there's nothing to do at night. The White House has set a new tone in making it an agreeable and fashionable civic duty to encourage the arts."

A consummate hostess, Jacqueline Kennedy revealed her taste in telling touches such as the introduction of convivial round tables seating eight or ten in place of the formidable horseshoe and giant E-shaped tables of years past. These she set with naturalistic flower arrangements and Madeleine Porthault's superb embroidered linen tablecloths, juxtaposed with the simple elegance of glassware from West Virginia (a state whose poverty had haunted her on the campaign trail). The menus were conceived by René Verdon, the talented French chef appointed by the Kennedys.

Jacqueline Kennedy's choice of clothing for an event was as deliberate as every other element of the evening, complementing and giving further physical expression to the Continental refinement of her entertaining. Mrs. Kennedy managed her public wardrobe as if she were a costume designer in theater or film; each outfit served to reinforce a point. For her daytime engagements at the White House she dressed with a studied and distinguished understatement, while at night her clothing became more evidently symbolic. Face to face with the Trumans, she was a dashing, modern metaphor for the Kennedy administration itself. For an audience with the Mona Lisa, however, her Empire gown established her as the romantic historicist that she patently was. These instinctive gestures reflected the fact that, as Richard Martin, the late curator of the Metropolitan Museum's Costume Institute, observed, "her style was not vanity but a way of living, not simply adorning herself but expressing her vision of beauty in the world."

White House

Chez Ninon (American, established ca. 1927), after fall–winter 1961 model by Marc Bohan (French, born 1926) for Christian Dior (French, established 1947). Two-piece day dress in dark red wool bouclé by Rodier, 1961. Opening of the Tutankhamun exhibition, National Gallery of Art, Washington, D.C., November 3, 1961. Televised tour of the White House, February 14, 1962. □ Chez Ninon was an exclusive Park Avenue custom dressmaking establishment run by Nona Park and Sophie Shonnard. Park and Shonnard (who had opened their salon in the late 1920s and had managed the made-to-measure department at Bonwit Teller in the forties and early fifties) were celebrated above all for the luxurious finesse of their European couture copies. Carmel Snow, editor in chief of *Harper's Bazaar,* considered them the most discerning American store buyers of Parisian fashion. The overblouse dress that Jacqueline Kennedy wore when she guided an estimated 56 million television viewers through the newly restored White House was a Chez Ninon line-for-line adaptation of "Passeport," a model in Marc Bohan's Dior collection. The premium paid to the couture houses to reproduce their models allowed Chez Ninon to use the fabric (Rodier's wool bouclé) and the buttons of Bohan's original; their skilled workrooms were able to copy details such as the thick chain-stitching outlining both the standaway neckline (into which Jacqueline Kennedy tucked her triple-strand artificial pearls) and the hem of the skirt that was one of Bohan's signatures for the house. The exaggerated asymmetry of the dress, dramatically highlighted by the placement of the buttons, references the bravura statements of Christian Dior's own midcentury collections. Bohan updated the effect, however, with the illusion of an unfitted bodice (standing away from the close fit of the underbodice) and a briskly abbreviated A-line skirt. □ Mrs. Kennedy was filmed at the White House over a three-day period in January 1962 for a Valentine's Day broadcast featuring the thirty-two-year-old first lady explaining in detail the history of the executive mansion, its rooms, and their contents. Much of the furniture and artwork on display, she pointed out, was only recently acquired through the efforts of the Fine Arts Committee for the White House and the generosity of donors from around the world, many of whom she thanked during the program. □ "It just seemed to me such a shame when we came here to find hardly anything of the past in the house, hardly anything before 1902," said Mrs. Kennedy, explaining her motivations for the project. "I know that when we went to Colombia, the Presidential Palace there had all the history of that country in it—where Simón Bolívar was—every piece of furniture in it has some link with the past. I thought the White House should be like that." □ Close to the end of the hour-long presentation, the president joined Mrs. Kennedy and CBS's Charles Collingwood, who had conducted the interview, and thanked the first lady for her efforts. "I have always felt that American history is sometimes a dull subject. There's so much emphasis on dates. But I think if [young students] can come here and see . . . this building and—in a sense—touch the people who have been here, then they'll go home more interested. I think they'll become better Americans. Some of them may want to someday live here themselves—which I think would be very good." □ Charles Collingwood later wrote to the first lady with the assurance that when the filming was over, "everyone from the lowliest porter to the director and producer felt they had been involved in one of the landmarks of this infant business."

Hubert de Givenchy. Dress in beige wool jersey with black kid sash belt, fall–winter 1959. Model number 2656. Receiving a season ticket for the National Symphony Orchestra, the White House, October 5, 1961. □ "Givenchy makes one exception to his policy of containment," wrote *Harper's Bazaar* to accompany a Richard Avedon photograph of this dress in the November 1959 issue, and there is a Chanel-inspired ease to this apparently unstructured dress (and choice of fabric) that was atypical of the designer's collections at the time. □ Givenchy presented an example of haute couture illusion in what appears to be a simple wrap dress. In fact, the fold of the skirt's "wrap" hides a deep pleat. His workroom technicians also contrived to give form to the pliant jersey; the collar's tailored roll was achieved by elaborate pick-stitching, a technique generally reserved for the unyielding fabric of a man's collar. For decorum's sake, Mrs. Kennedy wore her collar so that it broke higher than Givenchy originally showed it.

Oleg Cassini, after Hubert de Givenchy. Day ensemble of tunic and skirt in yellow silk crepe Giselle by Ascher, 1962. Diplomatic reception, the White House, May 2, 1962. □ Here, the Cassini workrooms created a line-for-line adaptation of an earlier Givenchy dress in embossed black silk organza that Jacqueline Kennedy owned (below). Thus reinterpreted in a more fluid fabric and an arresting color, the dress was transformed by Cassini from an archetypal Parisian "little black dress" into one calculated to stand out from the crowd. (A tunic with flying panels designed to fall into a graceful ascot-scarf drape in back provided further talking-point sophistication.) Mrs. Kennedy later transformed this dress once again, as well as the black Givenchy model, adapting the closures so that they could be used as maternity wear. □ The Kennedys reinvented many of the White House's traditionally white-tie events as "cocktail-champagne-buffet-dancing affair[s]," as the New York *Times* magazine of May 13, 1962, noted, adding that the atmosphere was "less formal, thus more relaxed, thus more fun." Above, they pose for photographers with Vice President and Mrs. Johnson.

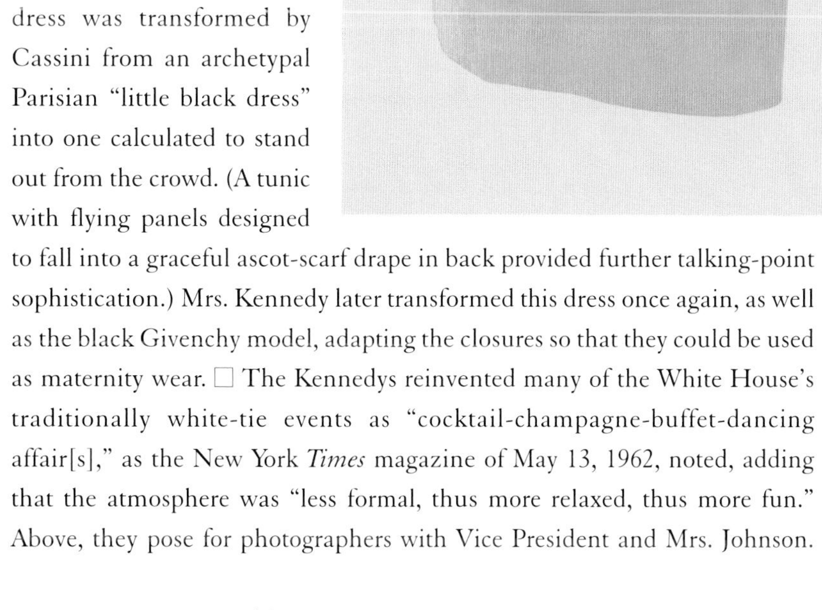

Oleg Cassini. Short evening suit in garnet silk velvet, 1963. Reception celebrating the centenary of the Emancipation Proclamation, the White House, February 12, 1963. Judicial reception, the White House, November 20, 1963. □ After their earlier emphatic fashion statements, this understated suit reveals a shift in focus for the collaboration between Jacqueline Kennedy and Oleg Cassini. Contributing to its relaxed Chanel feeling is a gilt chain—a characteristic device of that designer—which was sewn into the hem in the back of the jacket to weight and anchor it. Cassini relied for effect on the luxurious fabric and miniaturized his trademark buttons into delicate jet examples with a nineteenth-century flavor. □ A century after Abraham Lincoln issued the Emancipation Proclamation, President and Mrs. Kennedy hosted a White House reception (on the sixteenth president's birthday rather than on the official centenary, January 1) that was attended by the nation's civil rights leaders, among them Thurgood Marshall, Roy Wilkins, James Farmer, and Whitney Young Jr. Nine months later she wore the same suit to a judicial reception at which she was photographed standing between her husband and Chief Justice Earl Warren, with his wife (above).

White House

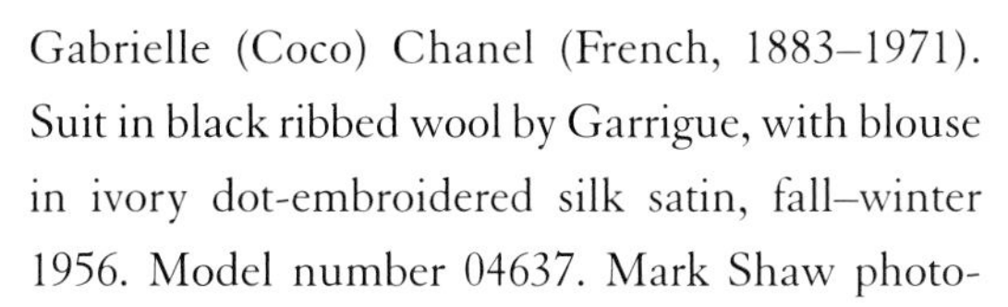

Gabrielle (Coco) Chanel (French, 1883–1971). Suit in black ribbed wool by Garrigue, with blouse in ivory dot-embroidered silk satin, fall–winter 1956. Model number 04637. Mark Shaw photographic sitting, Georgetown, Washington, D.C., 1958. Tour for officials of the American National Theater, the White House, March 12, 1963. □ Chanel reopened her couture house in 1954, after an extended hiatus that had begun with the outbreak of war. This was her feisty response to the "fifties horrors" that the male-dominated postwar couture world was producing. With its focus on modish exaggerations and dramatic seasonal changes, that world was antithetical to Chanel's own aesthetic and philosophy, which depended instead on essential principles of ease and timeless elegance and a sure sense that clothing should be subsidiary to the wearer. Initially reviled for her reeditions of her understated clothes that had once been so dominant, Chanel was championed by influential members of the American fashion press, including *Vogue*'s Bettina Ballard and *Life*'s Sally Kirkland, and lived to see her ideas embraced by new generations of women. Chanel's style precepts accorded perfectly with Jacqueline Kennedy's own vision. As a senator's wife she wore Chanel and continued to acquire the effortless but luxurious clothes as first lady. □ This suit embraces the idea of transformation that made Chanel's clothing a sensible couture investment; Jacqueline Kennedy wore it for at least seven years in both day and evening situations. In the designer's trademark manner, the jacket is lined in the same fabric as the blouse, and the blouse's cuffs are a trompe l'oeil; when the jacket is removed, a sleeveless shell is revealed.

Gabrielle (Coco) Chanel. Coat in ivory wool tweed with gilt buttons, spring–summer 1962. Model number 17133. Performance by the Pipes and Drums of the Black Watch, Royal Highland Regiment of the British Army, the White House, November 13, 1963. □ Chanel's deft workmanship—on this coat, the evenly spaced, horizontal rows of stitching—gave form and body to the loose-weave tweed that the designer delighted in using. The plain central panel on which she centered a quartet of her signature lion's-head buttons (suggesting the zodiac sign that she shared with the first lady) provided visual relief. In its crisp precision and deceptive rigidity of form, the coat is a reminder of Chanel's own delight in uniforms, and it served as a playful complement to the English Harris-tweed coats that the Kennedy children wore on this occasion. □ On this November afternoon President and Mrs. Kennedy, Caroline, and John joined 1,700 Washington-area children for a performance by the Pipes and Drums of the Black Watch. The first family watched the demonstration from the Truman Balcony off the White House second floor. They later greeted their guests and members of the regiment on the South Lawn before inviting all into the State Dining Room for hot chocolate and cookies.

Hubert de Givenchy, for Givenchy Boutique. Evening dress in ivory daisy-embroidered silk, 1960. Richard Avedon photographic sitting with John F. Kennedy Jr., Palm Beach, Florida, January 5, 1961. ☐ The hostess gown, or *déshabillé,* was a Givenchy staple and a favorite of Mrs. Kennedy's for its practicality and comfort. In fact, she wrote to Oleg Cassini's studio to suggest that he add this type of gown to his line. ☐ Givenchy stripped the decoration from the front of this dress, concentrating it in the back instead, where a fichu with a fringed trim merges artfully into the armhole. By alluding to the silhouette of the 1780s, Givenchy appealed to his client's sense of history. Mrs. Kennedy wore this dress for a Richard Avedon portrait with her newborn baby, John, which appeared in *Harper's Bazaar*'s February 1961 issue.

Bergdorf Goodman. Dress and jacket in deep pink silk matelassé, 1958. Wedding of Edward M. Kennedy and Virginia Joan Bennett, Bronxville, New York, November 29, 1958. Staff Christmas reception, the White House, December 13, 1961.

☐ In November 1960 Jacqueline Kennedy had considered entrusting Bergdorf Goodman with her wardrobe needs as first lady, and this ensemble (first worn to the 1958 wedding of Edward M. Kennedy and Virginia Joan Bennett) reveals something of the attraction that arrangement would have presented for her. Externally a model of simplicity, the dress was designed to throw into relief the luxurious silk matelassé with which it was made. It is the interior of the garment, however, that exemplifies the skill and exacting standards of Bergdorf's couture workrooms: the dress is lined in silk organza, nylon crinoline supports the hipline, and the exposed seams are finished with meticulous hand stitching. Mrs. Kennedy ultimately transferred her allegiance to Oleg Cassini and confined her planned Bergdorf's order to the inaugural ball ensemble. However, Bergdorf's custom millinery department and its inspired designer, Roy Halston Frowick, continued to provide most of the first lady's hats. ☐ Jacqueline Kennedy wore this outfit again to the 1961 Christmas party honoring the White House staff. The first couple posed for photographs in front of the Blue Room Christmas tree (painted by Mrs. Kennedy, above right) before circulating among their guests throughout the various state rooms.

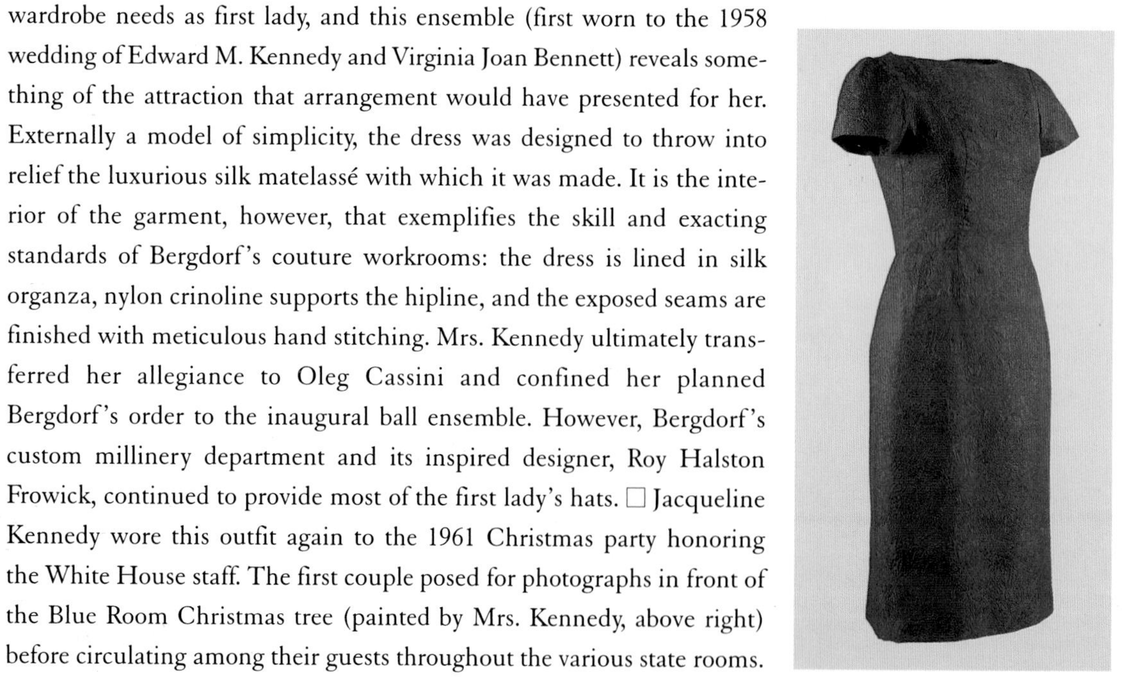

Hubert de Givenchy. Short evening dress in deep pink silk radzimir, fall–winter 1960. Model number 3118. Staff Christmas reception, the White House, December 12, 1962. □ In his characteristic style, Givenchy minimized detail on the front of this dress (although the armorial fit of the bodice and soft trumpet flare of the skirt are effects not easily achieved), while engaging in a flurry of sophisticated detailing in the back. Here, the magnificent ribbed-weave shot-silk fabric was manipulated into complex twists of drapery and neatly finished with a bow that requires the services of a lady's maid to tie. □ *Women's Wear Daily* sketched Princess Radziwill in this dress attending a ballet at Manhattan's City Center in March 1961. Jacqueline Kennedy and her ineffably stylish sister often exchanged clothes, and the first lady wore the dress, its drapery treatment so appropriately suggestive of a luxuriously wrapped gift, for the Kennedys' second Christmas reception for White House staff. □ President and Mrs. Kennedy posed for photographs in front of a sixteen-foot Christmas tree decked with miniature toys, candy canes, and gingerbread houses. Together with their 1,200 guests, they were serenaded by Air Force, Army, and Navy choral groups; the Marine Band provided musical accompaniment to the carols. □ Each White House employee received an autographed reproduction of a watercolor depicting the restored Red Room. The original was one of a series of depictions of the restored state rooms commissioned by Mrs. Kennedy from Pennsylvania artist Edward Lehman. Lehman's work first came to her attention when the Philadelphia *Inquirer* used his sleek pen-and-ink studies to illustrate an article on the progress of the first lady's White House project.

Oleg Cassini. Evening dress in ivory duchesse silk satin, 1961. Dinner honoring President and Mrs. Harry S. Truman, the White House, November 1, 1961. □ Jacqueline Kennedy was acutely sensitive to the symbolism of dress. At a dinner for Harry Truman (the first White House event honoring the former president since his return to private life in 1953), her choice of a relentlessly unembellished gown in the austere Balenciaga tradition cast her as a streamlined vision of modernity, the physical embodiment of the New Frontier. In the official photographic lineup the contrast that she presented with Bess Truman was dramatic. Intriguingly, Mrs. Truman was the first lady whom Jacqueline Kennedy most admired, "because she kept her family together in the White House regardless of the limelight that suddenly hits a President." □ After the dinner the pianist Eugene List, who had performed for President Truman, Winston Churchill, and Joseph Stalin at the Potsdam Conference in 1945, presented a selection of the ex-president's favorite Chopin pieces. Later, Truman, a keen amateur pianist, played Paderewski's Minuet in G.

Oleg Cassini. Evening gown in ivory silk ziberline embroidered with jet beads, and capelet in ivory silk ziberline, 1961. Dinner hosted by President Manuel Prado, Embassy of Peru, Washington, D.C., September 21, 1961. State dinner for Prime Minister Jawaharlal Nehru of India, the White House, November 7, 1961. □ Cassini reduced the ball gown to its simplest elements: a bell-shaped skirt blooming from a tight, spare bodice. The decoration is restricted to the bodice and could be hidden, on arrival, beneath a shaped capelet. In lieu of cumbersome evening coats, Jacqueline Kennedy often requested wraps and stoles that could be worn with ease or gracefully discarded, as desired. □ She wore this dress at a small official dinner for Prime Minister Nehru of India and his daughter, Indira Gandhi. The Kennedys first entertained Nehru and his daughter privately at Hammersmith Farm, the Rhode Island estate where they had been married, which was owned by Jacqueline Kennedy's mother and stepfather, Janet and Hugh Auchincloss. They then flew on to Washington, arriving by helicopter on the White House lawn, for the evening's festivities. □ Mrs. Kennedy had also worn the dress in September at a dinner given by President Prado of Peru and his wife at the Peruvian embassy in Washington. That time, she had transformed the dress for the purposes of the official photograph (above) by wearing it with its little cape. A Washington journalist characterized Señora Prado's dress as "what has come to be known as a 'Jackie creation' . . . a slim two-piece, sleeveless sheath."

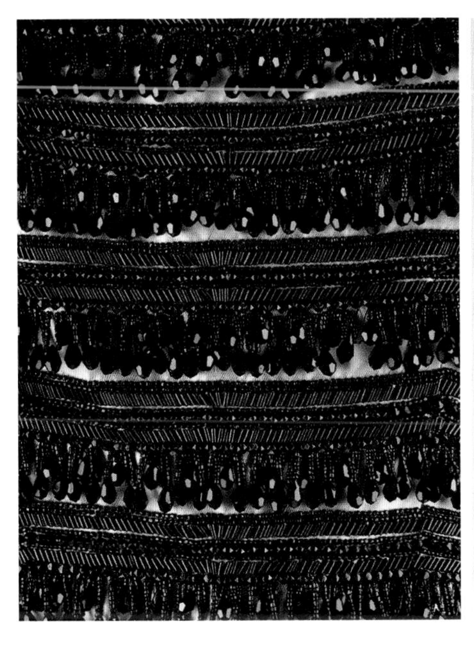

Oleg Cassini. Evening skirt and jacket in chartreuse silk faille with shell top embroidered with crystal beads and sequins, 1961. State dinner honoring Governor Luis Muñoz Marín of Puerto Rico, the White House, November 13, 1961. Dinner hosted by Ambassador and Mrs. John Kenneth Galbraith, Jaipur, India, March 19, 1962. □ In many of her evening choices Jacqueline Kennedy achieved a degree of traditional splendor with a modern simplification of elements. Here, she and Cassini reduced the formal evening ensemble to three easy pieces. The beaded shell, with her preferred formula of a modest bateau neckline and unusual back detail, was cut short to attenuate the stemlike form of the lean skirt. With this, Cassini provided the option of an abbreviated evening jacket. □ For a dinner honoring Puerto Rico's chief executive, Governor Muñoz Marín, and his wife, President Kennedy personally invited the legendary Spanish cellist Pablo Casals, then eighty-five years old and living in exile in Puerto Rico, to perform. Casals had played at the White House before—in 1904 for President Theodore Roosevelt. When the U.S. government later recognized the Fascist regime of Generalissimo Franco, Casals had vowed never again to make music in America. As he was an admirer of the president and a close friend of the governor, however, he agreed to perform but chose not to accept the invitation to dinner, which might have given the impression that he had compromised his political ideals. Casals played selections from the works of Mendelssohn, Schumann, and Couperin for an evening that the New York *Times* observed was "an indication that the White House was rising to its responsibility and . . . coming of age." □ Appropriately, the guest list included many of America's most celebrated composers and conductors, among them Samuel Barber, Aaron Copland, Gian Carlo Menotti, Leonard Bernstein, Leopold Stokowski, and Virgil Thomson, as well as Harry Belafonte and Mrs. Nicholas Longworth, President Roosevelt's daughter, who had been present at Casals's White House concert more than half a century earlier. Before the historic performance President Kennedy said, "I think it is most important not that we regard artistic achievement and action as a part of our armor in these difficult days, but rather as an integral part of our free society." □ In her letter of thanks to Mrs. Kennedy, Marta Casals praised the president who "represents with such dignity both cultural and human idealisms of a free world" and wrote that for her husband, the evening had represented "the strengthening of the artistic and human ideals that have always inspired his life."

Chez Ninon, after fall–winter 1961 model by Jules-François Crahay (French, 1917–1988) for Nina Ricci (French, established 1932). Evening dress in black silk velvet and Chinese yellow silk satin, 1961. State dinner honoring President Manuel Prado of Peru, the White House, September 19, 1961. □ Jules-François Crahay enjoyed notable success as the designer for Nina Ricci between 1954 and 1963. Nicole Alphand, the French ambassador's chic wife, whose style Jacqueline Kennedy much admired, was a devotee. Crahay would later design for Lanvin, where his collections were noted for the ethnic excursions in which he indulged. Here, he went no farther than the Spain of Goya for a dramatic dress that, as Jacqueline Kennedy's social secretary, Letitia Baldrige, has noted, was a particular favorite of the president's. □ The dress was originally designed with the bodice in deep brown, a color that the first lady never cared for. Reinterpreted in black and Chinese yellow, it promised to stand out even more dramatically in the State Dining Room, just repainted off-white—a detail that Mrs. Kennedy might well have considered. □ Jacqueline Kennedy bought this dress at Chez Ninon, where workroom skills were exemplified in such telling details as the hand-knotted fringe of the sash. The straight, high neckline emphasized her collarbone, and *Women's Wear Daily,* which ran an illustration of the dress on November 19, noted that it "daringly plunged to her waist at back." □ After the state dinner for President Prado of Peru, his fashionable wife (wearing Dior), and ninety guests, the Metropolitan Opera stars Roberta Peters and Jerome Hines performed selections from *The Barber of Seville* and *Porgy and Bess* in the East Room. In spite of their shared love of ceremony, the Kennedys introduced an air of luxurious informality into the traditionally rigid atmosphere of White House entertaining. Breaking with White House precedent on this occasion, the president introduced members of the press to the guests of honor and then invited the reporters to mingle with the group; in another departure from tradition, the ladies did not withdraw after dinner but remained to share coffee and liqueurs with the gentlemen.

Oleg Cassini. Evening dress in celadon silk jersey, 1962. Dinner honoring Nobel prizewinners of the Western Hemisphere, the White House, April 29, 1962. □ "COGNOSCENTI COME TO CALL . . . A brilliant night to remember at the White House," trumpeted *Life* of the April evening on which the Kennedys entertained forty-nine Nobel laureates and other distinguished guests drawn from the worlds of education, science, and the arts, including Pearl Buck, Robert Frost, James Baldwin, Mrs. Ernest Hemingway, Linus Pauling, and Katherine Anne Porter, as well as the astronaut John H. Glenn Jr. After dinner the Academy Award–winning actor Fredric March read from the writings of American Nobelists Sinclair Lewis, General George C. Marshall, and Ernest Hemingway. □ At the beginning of the year Jacqueline Kennedy had suggested to Cassini that draped jersey "would be fun for a change." Cassini obliged with an atypical creation in the jersey fabric that Madame Grès had developed in the 1930s for her signature draperies *à l'antique*. Cassini's liquid, columnar dress was also suggestive of ancient statuary. It was entirely appropriate that for this shining hour, which recognized and celebrated excellence in the fields of science, peace, and literature, Jacqueline Kennedy cast herself as the dynamic modern embodiment of an ancient muse. □ Author William Styron later wrote in *Vanity Fair* of the Kennedys' entrance that "Jack and Jackie actually *shimmered*. . . . even Republicans were gaga." In a marvelously evocative and elegiac memoir of the evening, published in *The New Yorker* in 1997, Diana Trilling also recalled the moment that the president and first lady entered to "a great fanfare of trumpets. . . . They had just come back from the Palm Beach vacation, and they were very suntanned. Jackie was a deep cocoa brown and she was wearing a sea-green chiffon dress, to the floor, but cut very simply except that it had one bare shoulder. She wore green slippers to match her dress and no jewelry at all except some earrings, which were the most beautiful shade of green. She was a hundred times more beautiful than any photograph ever indicated."

Guy Douvier (French, 1928–1993), for Christian Dior. Evening dress in candy pink silk-dupioni shantung, 1962. State dinner honoring André Malraux, France's minister of culture, the White House, May 11, 1962. □ Christian Dior, quick to understand and exploit the magic of his name, had established a New York licensing outpost in 1949. In the early 1960s Guy Douvier was its in-house designer. Although he sometimes borrowed elements from Marc Bohan's keynote Paris couture collections for Dior, Douvier's own brisk designs were more specific to an American clientele. The company's press officer at the time, Mary McFadden, personally delivered several Dior–New York pieces to Jacqueline Kennedy at the White House (McFadden, after changing professions, would design clothes for her later in life). This gown, originally shown in yellow, was chosen for Jacqueline Kennedy by her sister, Lee Radziwill, and Diana Vreeland, with whom Radziwill had once worked at *Harper's Bazaar.* The stylish and sophisticated Radziwill was an important fashion scout for the first lady. Presenting a strictly unembellished line in front, the dress wraps into a toga drape in the back, where it is anchored with a stiff Kabuki bow. Although its construction techniques lack the precision and finesse of a Paris original, the dress relies on such Diorisms as a boned, cotton-net underbodice that contains the figure, allowing the silk to glide over the top. □ The Kennedys greatly admired André Malraux as a cultural evangelist. By according him the courtesies normally reserved for a head of state, they sought to focus national attention on the role of the arts in America. (Jacqueline Kennedy would hold him as a model when she lobbied to create an American secretary for the arts at the cabinet level.) The first lady carefully compiled a guest list to reflect Malraux's multifaceted career as a novelist (*La condition humaine,* or *Man's Fate,* of 1933 was his masterpiece), art historian (*The Voices of Silence,* 1951), explorer, resistance fighter, and statesman. She particularly sought out American artists whose work was applauded in France, including Mark Rothko, Leonard Bernstein, Arthur Miller, Robert Lowell, Saul Bellow, Elia Kazan, George Balanchine, Lee Strasberg, Thornton Wilder, Julie Harris, Tennessee Williams, and Geraldine Page. The reclusive aviator Charles Lindbergh and his wife, the writer Anne Morrow Lindbergh, were the cause of particular excitement. In a memo about the guest list Jacqueline Kennedy noted that, for the Malraux evening, Lindbergh "would be great as he landed in France." □ Before this illustrious crowd the president affirmed that "'creativity' is the hardest work there is" and playfully said that the White House was "becoming a sort of eating place for artists. But they never ask us out." In her letter of thanks Julie Harris noted that the evening "meant a great deal to us in the Arts and Theatre," and Geraldine Page wrote, "I may never recover," admitting that she had decided to "gush and be damned." Her letter continued, "I had the sensation at your party of being a simple blossom in a huge field of flowers all basking in the sun so we could hold up our heads and be beautiful." But perhaps the greatest compliment of all came from the honoree, who, at the end of the dinner, whispered a promise to Jacqueline Kennedy that he would send to her France's most famous cultural treasure, *La Gioconda*—the Mona Lisa.

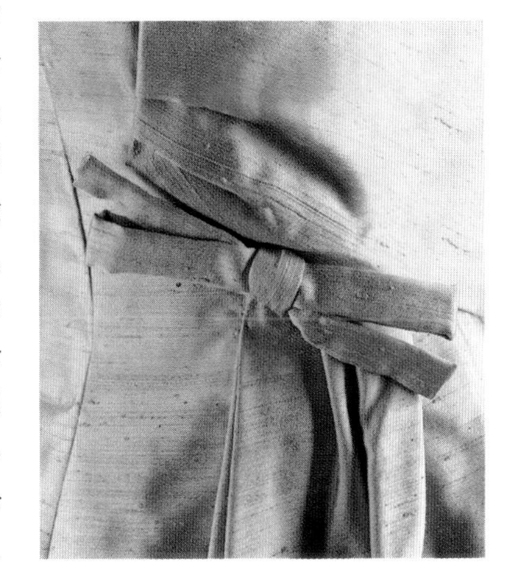

Oleg Cassini, after Karl Lagerfeld (German, born 1938) for Jean Patou (French, established 1919). Evening dress in silver-spangled white synthetic tulle embroidered with rhinestones and trimmed with gray silk velvet, 1962. State dinner honoring President Félix Houphouët-Boigny of the Ivory Coast, the White House, May 22, 1962. □ As Jacqueline Kennedy moved away from the severe Givenchy aesthetic, she allowed herself more romantic gestures. This fairy-tale dress is based on a design by Karl Lagerfeld, who had been the couturier at Jean Patou since 1960. Lagerfeld's original was photographed in *Harper's Bazaar* (April 1962) and in *L'Officiel* (March 1962), both magazines to which Mrs. Kennedy subscribed. It reflected Lagerfeld's enduring interest in the fashions of the immediate pre–World War I period and in the illustrations of Paul Iribe and Georges Lepape, who had recorded the clothes of Paul Poiret and his contemporaries with such exquisite grace. The Cassini atelier created an effective reproduction, with laborious embroidery and appropriate fabric substitutions. The detailing, however, is at variance with Parisian standards. Bordering the bodice and hem, for instance, are bands of net that were embroidered before being applied to the finished garment. In a Paris couture atelier the embroidery would have been worked directly on the panels of the dress itself before it was fully assembled, thus becoming an integral part of the gown rather than an applied element. All Mrs. Kennedy required, however, was a dress that was perfectly photogenic, and Cassini's served this purpose effectively. □ As colonialism receded, the Kennedy administration took particular care to acknowledge the leaders of newly independent states in Africa. The president himself had a special interest in the continent and was known there for his outspoken opposition to colonial rule. One of twenty-eight official events honoring the leaders of emerging African nations was the state dinner for President and Madame Houphouët-Boigny of the Ivory Coast. Madame Houphouët-Boigny, dubbed "Africa's Jackie," lived up to her reputation in an embroidered satin gown by Pierre Balmain. (Together, she and Jacqueline Kennedy graced the cover of the August 1962 issue of *Ebony*.) The after-dinner entertainment was a performance by the American Ballet Theatre of *Billy the Kid,* with music by Aaron Copland, one of the dinner guests.

Oleg Cassini. Evening dress in black Fortuny-pleated silk satin charmeuse, 1962. State dinner for President Rómulo Betancourt of Venezuela, the White House, February 19, 1963. □ "Jackie reminded me of an Egyptian princess," Oleg Cassini has recalled—"very geometric, even hieroglyphic, with the sphinx-like quality of her eyes, her long neck, slim torso, broad shoulders, narrow hips, and regal carriage." Perhaps with these sentiments in mind, Cassini designed a dress for her that was a stylish modernization of Irene Sharaff's costumes for Elizabeth Taylor in the movie *Cleopatra,* then laboring in its third year of filming. □ For the "Cleopatra of the Potomac" (a contemporary journalist's sobriquet), Cassini created a dramatic garment that reflected his preference for voluptuous, body-revealing fashion statements. Mrs. Kennedy evidently appreciated the effect and had a variant made in white that she would wear for a New Year's Eve soiree at the Charles Wrightsmans. □ The February evening at the White House was another departure from the traditional formality of entertaining the visiting head of a foreign government, as President and Mrs. Rómulo Betancourt of Venezuela and thirty-two other guests were invited to the family dining room on the first floor. As the Washington *Evening Star* reported, "the small, intimate dinner seemed to underscore the open admiration felt by the Kennedy administration for this champion of democracy."

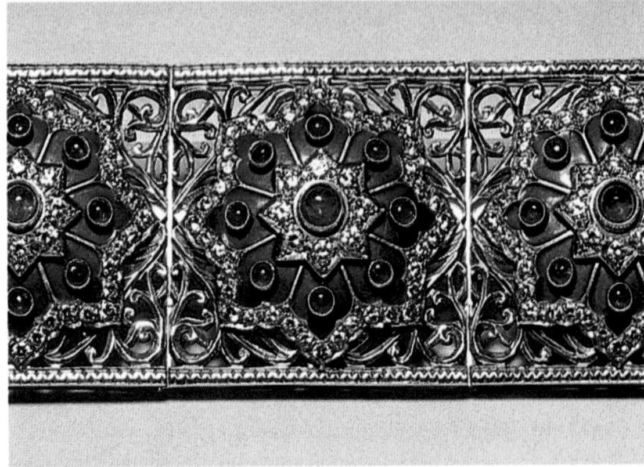

Oleg Cassini. Evening dress in ivory silk crepe with matching cardigan jacket (not shown), 1963. Posing for photographs in the Yellow Oval Room, the White House, March 28, 1963. □ This ensemble presents two different aspects. Worn with the dress's bow showing at the neck of the prim cardigan jacket, it is a model of propriety. When the jacket is removed, however, the dress is revealed to be daringly cut away from its halter-tie neck. Mrs. Kennedy's ensemble was based on one in Cassini's Young America collection; the designer was assiduous and forward-thinking in his pursuit of licensing agreements and development of secondary lines. □ For Jacqueline Kennedy, the stark simplicity of the dress proved a perfect foil for the magnificently jeweled, filigreed gold bracelet (above) and belt presented to her by King Hassan II of Morocco at a state dinner given in his honor the night before the Yellow Oval Room photo session.

Oleg Cassini, after spring–summer 1962 model by Federico Forquet (Italian, born 1931). Evening dress in mauve silk gazar, 1963. State dinner honoring Grand Duchess Charlotte of Luxembourg, the White House, April 30, 1963. □ For a dinner to honor the grand duchess of Luxembourg, Jacqueline Kennedy presented a briskly updated Edwardian vision. The emerging Roman couturier Federico Forquet had made the "umbrella over-skirt" (illustrated in *Women's Wear Daily* on March 13, 1962) a motif of his spring–summer 1962 collection; Nina Ricci's Jules-François Crahay explored a similar effect in an evening dress photographed in *L'Art et la mode* in March 1962. Evidently, it was an idea that was in the air. Cassini's own variant is in a soft Belle Epoque mauve; the ruffled waist disguised the first lady's incipient pregnancy (this was her last official appearance before the birth of her son Patrick). Cassini's use of gazar—a rigid silk weave developed by the fabric house Abraham for Balenciaga—gives an emphatic structure to the dress. Kenneth counterpointed this by placing Mrs. Kennedy's antique diamond starburst (found at Wartski's in London) in her hair, in the mid-nineteenth-century manner popularized by Elizabeth of Austria. Happily, Luxembourg's monarch dressed her part to perfection, too. The Washington *Post* noted that she "looked exactly as most Hollywood movie studios would cast the ruler of a picture postcard land. . . . She trailed [Jean Dessès's] white chiffon draperies beneath a frosty mink capelet." □ The first lady had learned that the grand duchess was a Shakespeare enthusiast and so orchestrated an evening of early-seventeenth-century entertainments that included performances by the Consort Players on contemporary instruments and readings from Shakespeare, Marlowe, and Jonson by Basil Rathbone in "the old-fashioned oratorical style," as the Washington *Evening Star* observed. Mrs. Kennedy asked that Rathbone include her favorite sonnets and close the evening with Henry V's Saint Crispin's Day speech, the president's favorite Shakespearean text. The president knew it by heart, which, Rathbone admitted, "scared the daylights out of" him. □ The grand duchess, in her own tribute, called Jacqueline Kennedy "America's most potent weapon, Madame *La Présidente*."

Chez Ninon, after fall–winter 1961 model number 124 by Antonio Castillo (Spanish, 1908–1984) for Lanvin (French, established 1889). Evening dress in ivory duchesse silk satin and ruby-beaded silk organdy, 1961. Dinner hosted by Prime Minister Jawaharlal Nehru, Indian Embassy, Washington, D.C., November 9, 1961. Dinner hosted by Ambassador John Kenneth Galbraith, U.S. Embassy, New Delhi, March 20, 1962. Fund-raiser celebrating the second anniversary of the Kennedy inauguration, National Guard Armory, Washington, D.C., January 18, 1963. □ Prime Minister Nehru traditionally wore a rosebud boutonniere in his eponymous jacket, and it was perhaps in elegant recognition of this fact that Jacqueline Kennedy wore this dress, with its rose-covered bodice, in his presence on two different occasions. The dress was acquired through Chez Ninon, whose buyers announced to *Women's Wear Daily* that they had the first lady in mind when they selected it in Paris. Antonio Castillo had worked for Elizabeth Arden's custom salon in New York in the 1940s, and later for Paquin, before linking his name with Jeanne Lanvin's in 1950. At Lanvin his clothes were distinguished for their quiet luxury and conservative restraint, as exemplified by this dress, with its tone-on-tone beaded bodice and softly belling skirt. □ Chez Ninon made frank couture copies, and there was always a danger that other clients would have the same dress, acquired from this New York house or at source in Paris. In fact, Mitzi Newhouse, wife of the magazine tycoon Samuel Newhouse, wore her own version of this model (now in the collection of the Costume Institute) to the White House dinner for Nobel prizewinners on April 29, 1962.

Oleg Cassini. Evening dress in ivory duchesse silk satin and bolero in ivory duchesse silk satin embroidered by Brody with crystal beads and shells, 1962. Fund-raiser celebrating the first anniversary of the Kennedy inauguration, National Guard Armory, Washington, D.C., January 20, 1962. Dinner honoring Jacqueline Kennedy, New Delhi, March 13, 1962. □ The jewel-like embroidered bolero jacket was a mainstay of Paris couture in this period. Givenchy and Balenciaga used it constantly in partnership with dresses that were conspicuously unembellished. Cassini did the same thing here, juxtaposing the lavishly detailed bolero, its abstracted *botehs* (paisley whorls) outlined in tiny pearlescent shells, with a sleek satin dress. (Mrs. Kennedy, shown below left with Lady Pamela Hicks, wore the dress minus its jacket in India.) In the dress itself, Cassini combined tradition with modernity. While the flying panel in back lends it an almost imperial quality, this vestige of a court train was actually constructed with a light enough touch that, when Mrs. Kennedy sat down to dine, it could be flipped aside as easily as a man's tailcoat. □ The ensemble was another example of the luxurious detailing deployed with careful restraint that Jacqueline Kennedy found so compelling. She wore the jacket and dress to a fund-raiser for the Democratic Party at the National Guard Armory, where her dinner companion was the former president Harry S. Truman (right).

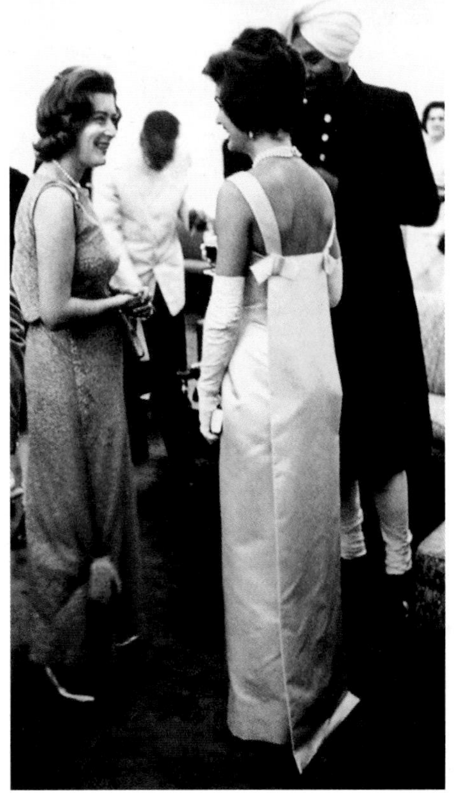

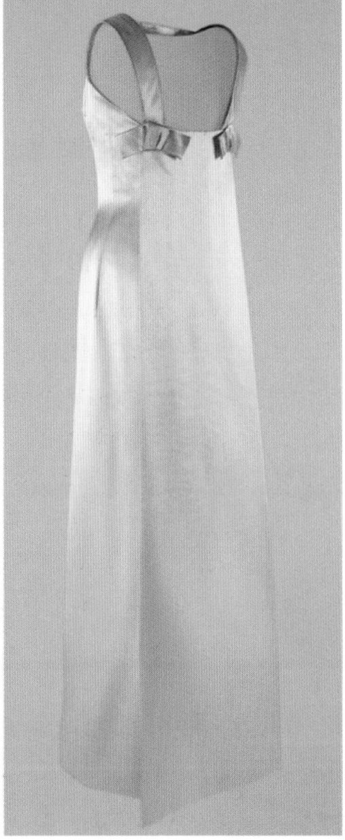

Oleg Cassini, after spring–summer 1962 model number 163 ("Théâtre de Verdure") by Marc Bohan for Christian Dior. Two-piece evening ensemble in pale green silk chiffon embroidered with sequins and rhinestones, 1962. Dinner hosted by President Félix Houphouët-Boigny of the Ivory Coast, Mayflower Hotel, Washington, D.C., May 24, 1962. □ The Cassini workrooms replicated a dress designed by Marc Bohan at Christian Dior. In the Dior original, named "Théâtre de Verdure," a photograph of which appeared in the March 1962 issue of *L'Officiel* (right), the vertical fern fronds of crystal-and-sequin embroidery were subtly tapered to feathery points at the top and bottom; a trellis of individually applied sequins was sewn on as an allover ground. In the Cassini interpretation the embroidery was skillfully accomplished, but instead of matching the poetic evanescence of the original, the stripes of sequins and beads end abruptly. □ Marc Bohan continued the Christian Dior tradition of luxurious femininity. The construction of Dior's evening clothes often involved a separate bodice and skirt in the nineteenth-century manner. However, where Dior generally linked the elements with a belt at a crisply defined waistline, Bohan modernized the concept with an overblouse effect that appealed to Jacqueline Kennedy's preference for clothing that skimmed, rather than defined, the body.

Washington

Joan Morse (American, 1932–1972), for A La Carte (American, established ca. 1962). Evening dress and cape in hot-pink-and-gold silk organza and metallic-brocaded silk organza, trimmed in olive silk velvet, 1962. Benefit performance of the musical *Mr. President* for the Joseph P. Kennedy Jr. Foundation, National Theatre, Washington, D.C., September 6, 1962. □ During his February 1962 visit to the White House, King Saud of Saudi Arabia presented the first lady with a length of magnificent silk brocade. She had this fabric made into an evening dress by A La Carte, a fashionable Manhattan boutique, whose designer Joan Morse was noted for the flamboyant clothes she made from fabrics collected on her world travels. Morse would later reinvent herself as "Tiger" and, in the words of Marilyn Bender, the New York *Times* fashion writer, become "La Pasionaria of the dropout subculture of pop." There is little in this dress to suggest the Morse wildness to come, although the exotic brocade does invest it with a prototypical hippie-deluxe quality—perfect for Jacqueline Kennedy, who once playfully signed a note to decorator Billy Baldwin "Mme Suleiman Le Brillant." □ She evidently liked this dress enough to have the original green velvet bodice replaced with one of pale organza, presumably for warmer weather. In its first incarnation she wore the dress to a charity benefit performance (for the Joseph P. Kennedy Jr. Foundation) of Irving Berlin's musical *Mr. President*. The Berlin musical opened "on an energetic twisting party" at the White House. It was a timely reference: Oleg Cassini claims to have introduced the twist to the White House at a dinner dance the Kennedys gave for the Radziwills, and he was inclined to punctuate his fashion shows with it.

Oleg Cassini, after spring–summer 1962 model number 3786 by Hubert de Givenchy (p. 31). Evening dress in pink silk chiffon with porcelain beads and rhinestones, 1963. Opening of the Mona Lisa exhibition, National Gallery of Art, Washington, D.C., January 8, 1963. State dinner honoring President Sarvepalli Radhakrishnan of India, the White House, June 3, 1963. □ Givenchy's original design was an intriguing synthesis of the sari—a fashion craze in the wake of Mrs. Kennedy's India tour and a motif of enduring interest to both Givenchy and Balenciaga—and the ersatz Edwardiana of *My Fair Lady*. In fact, modish Paris couture provided some reference points for Cecil Beaton as he developed the costumes for the movie in 1963, and Givenchy in turn might have been inspired by Beaton's work when he visited him on the set. □ Jacqueline Kennedy had noticed a Howell Conant photograph of Audrey Hepburn wearing the original (yellow) version of the dress in the May 11, 1962, issue of *Life,* and a Best Dressed friend had also thoughtfully supplied her with a sketch from the designer. With these references at hand, the Cassini workrooms successfully fulfilled their client's request. □ André Malraux accompanied the "most famous painting in the world" to Washington for a gala unveiling at the National Gallery of Art. The French government as well as the trustees of the Louvre had opposed the loan at first, concerned about the risk to this supreme national treasure. However, Malraux, in appreciation of the Kennedys' enthusiastic promotion of the arts in America, eventually secured the painting as a personal loan to President Kennedy. Nearly seven hundred thousand people saw it at the National Gallery, and more than a million when it was transferred to The Metropolitan Museum of Art. President Kennedy expressed his gratitude for the loan from "the world's leading artistic power," adding that "we will continue to press ahead to develop an independent artistic force and power of our own." For Mrs. Kennedy this was a personal triumph. "It was a long-awaited reunion," noted *Life*, "and both ladies were at their glowing best."

INDIA

Travel

Refuting the supposed parochialism of the United States in the postwar period, Jacqueline Kennedy presented America's new face—one that was cultured, sophisticated, and stylish—to the world. Her graceful internationalism, evidenced in her linguistic abilities and her informed interest in the culture and history of the countries she visited, was reinforced visually through her scrupulously constructed public image. Once more, clothing was to prove a striking metaphor for the first lady's role, in this case as an effective goodwill ambassador. The first intimations of Jacqueline Kennedy's potent impact on the world stage came on the president's first state trip, to Canada in May 1961. "The Canadians were screaming 'Jackie, Jackie' in the streets and Canadians just don't scream like that normally," remembered Letitia Baldrige, Jacqueline Kennedy's wry social secretary. "This was the beginning of her popularity and I think he really looked at her with new eyes on this occasion." If the Canadian reception introduced the president to the universality of his wife's appeal, the couple's European tour a month later was a dramatic confirmation of the phenomenon. At a press luncheon in Paris Kennedy famously diverged from his prepared speech to say, "I do not think it entirely inappropriate to introduce myself to this audience. I am the man who accompanied Jacqueline Kennedy to Paris, and I have enjoyed it!"

During her formative junior year studying in Grenoble and at the Sorbonne, Jacqueline Bouvier had been "galled at the patronizing attitude toward America, annoyed by the compliment 'but no one would think you were American,' if one showed a knowledge of literature and history." Returning to France as first lady was a vindication of her home country. Dressed by Givenchy, Cassini, and Chez Ninon, jeweled by Van Cleef and Arpels, with her hair arranged by Paris's preeminent coiffeur, Alexandre, she was a vision of unimpeachable elegance. She was also an adroit ambassador, occasionally acting as interpreter for her husband and Charles de Gaulle, whom she beguiled with her fluent conversation about French history and culture. In Vienna her coruscating appearance at Schönbrunn Palace had a visible impact on Nikita Khrushchev, somewhat diffusing the tensions that had arisen from an unproductive day of discussions between the U.S. president and the irascible Soviet premier.

Jacqueline Kennedy's televised tour of the White House on February 14, 1962, was broadcast internationally and further established her as a figure of world interest. In its wake she took a goodwill tour of India and Pakistan, accompanied by her sister, Lee Radziwill. In both, she was received as "America's Queen." In South America she was revered as a "folk heroine," according to Lincoln Gordon, the U.S. ambassador to Brazil, and her appearances elicited something akin to pop-icon adulation. In Venezuela, for instance, twenty thousand troops were on hand to control the crowds. Throughout, Jacqueline Kennedy used clothing as a theatrical device, dressing in subtle complement to her host nation. When she visited Versailles the Parisian couturier Givenchy was given due credit as the author of her fresh but regal ensemble. For a trip to Mexico Oleg Cassini created a collection of outfits for her in appropriate "sun colors." And for the tour of India and Pakistan Jacqueline Kennedy assembled a wardrobe from various fashion houses with the panache of a costume designer. Its vivid palette was that of Mughal miniatures, and the reflective fabrics conferred an additional brilliance. With such close attention to detail and sensitivity to sartorial effect, it was perhaps inevitable that concerted attempts to discourage reporters from focusing on her fashions were conspicuously unsuccessful. Far more significant, however, was Jacqueline Kennedy's ability to manipulate clothing into a striking visual metaphor for what she represented not just to Americans but to the world: the youthful promise of the Kennedy administration.

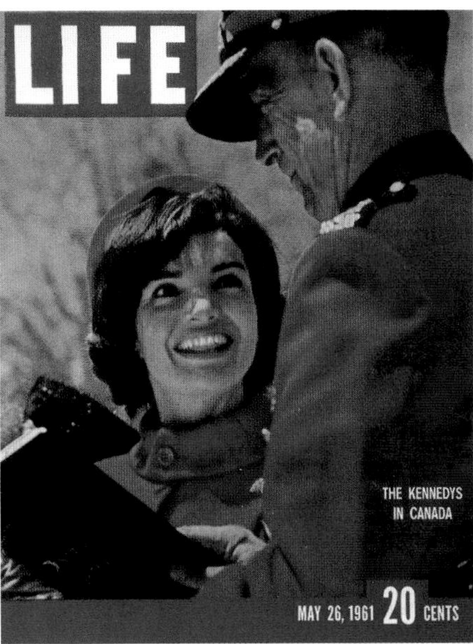

Pierre Cardin (French, born 1922). Day suit in red wool twill, ca. 1957. Visit to the barracks of the Royal Canadian Mounted Police, Ottawa, May 16, 1961. □ The sophisticated martial cut and strident coloration of this Cardin suit, which Jacqueline Kennedy wore on her triumphant international debut as first lady, were perceived as a stylish and calculated complement to the uniforms of the Royal Canadian Mounted Police. She had acquired the suit five years earlier and had worn it for a segment on NBC's "Home" show, billed as a "woman's magazine of the air." Hosted by Arlene Francis, the program, broadcast on April 3, 1957, tracked Mrs. Kennedy's daily rounds as a dutiful Georgetown housewife. □ In this period and through the early sixties, Cardin focused attention on elaborate back detailing, such as the twisted martingale half-belt in the back of the jacket (below right). The curving seams, which shape the body, the sleeves, and the back of the skirt betray Cardin's earlier career as a tailor at Christian Dior and point to his experiments in geometry, which would develop into the futurist look of his sixties work. In the late fifties, however, Cardin was celebrated for the jaunty, youthful elegance of his tailoring. Célia Bertin, writing in *Paris à la mode* in 1956, found the young designer "especially gifted in the cutting of tailor-mades" and a happy choice for a senator's style-conscious young wife (and for her sister, Lee Radziwill, who had the same suit in beige).

Oleg Cassini. Suit in pale yellow silk-and-wool Alaskine by Bucol, 1961. Easter Sunday, Palm Beach, Florida, April 2, 1961. Luncheon with President and Mme Charles de Gaulle at the Élysée Palace, Paris, May 31, 1961. Luncheon with Prime Minister Harold Macmillan, London, June 5, 1961. Accepting first copy of the White House guidebook, the White House, June 28, 1962. □ Halston, for Bergdorf Goodman. Hat of natural straw, 1961. Luncheon, Élysée Palace, Paris, May 31, 1961. □ Jacqueline Kennedy's preference for stiff and unyielding fabrics (such as this silk-and-wool blend called Alaskine, developed by the silk house Bucol) lends an armorial quality to much of her clothing from this period. By using such materials, Cassini gave his clothes emphatic form with a minimum of interior construction. There is an almost cartoonish abstraction to this understated suit, with its crisp A-line skirt and simple boxy jacket enlivened by a pocket which was placed off center and is thus purely ornamental. Halston contrived to create a hat with a brim that was really a surrogate pillbox, satisfying his client's need for unobtrusive headgear that would reveal her face to the public. □ This suit was a favorite of Mrs. Kennedy's, and its foreign debut was at a luncheon held at the Élysée Palace, official residence of the president of France, to welcome her to Paris. Later that day she accompanied Mme de Gaulle to the city's Institut de Puériculture, a nursery school that was of special interest to the French first lady.

Oleg Cassini. Evening dress in pink-and-white raffia lace with matching stole, 1961. Dinner at the Élysée Palace, Paris, May 31, 1961. □ A brilliant response to Jacqueline Kennedy's desire to project sophistication without ostentation on her first gala evening in France, this dress and its modest kerchief stole rely for impact almost entirely on the splendor of the elaborate pink-and-white lace that Diana Vreeland had recommended. The fabric dictated even the detailing of the dress, its scalloped edge providing a decorative flourish at the hem and armhole. The courtly implications of the lace were subverted by the humble material from which it was made: straw. To complement the purity of the dress, the celebrated coiffeur Alexandre created a graphic "Gothic Madonna" hairstyle inspired by a Carlo Crivelli painting. □ As journalist Mary Van Rensselaer Thayer noted of that evening, which unfolded in the eighteenth-century magnificence of the Élysée Palace, "Truly la vie was very much en rose." Three hundred guests enjoyed a dinner served on Sèvres china with Napoléon's vermeil flatware, and the orchestra of the Garde Républicaine performed a musical program that included Gershwin's *Rhapsody in Blue* and Ravel's *Boléro.* In his toast President Kennedy acknowledged his wife's skills as a goodwill ambassador, noting that "my preparation for the Presidency did not include acquiring first-hand knowledge of France through diplomatic experience. I acquired it through marriage instead."

Chez Ninon. Suit in navy silk shantung, 1961. Luncheon with Chief Mayor Julien Tardieu, Hôtel de Ville, Paris, June 1, 1961. Luncheon with Nina Khrushchev, Pallavicini Palace, Vienna, June 4, 1961. Ceremony bestowing honorary U.S. citizenship on Sir Winston Churchill, the White House, April 9, 1963. □ This suit is emblematic of the quiet elegance and propriety of Chez Ninon's clothes, whether derived directly from European couture sources or, as here, conceived by one of its in-house designers. On her return from Europe Jacqueline Kennedy wrote to her saleswoman at the house, Mrs. Tuckaberry (Molly) McAdoo, that she had been "so enchanted with the clothes for my trip" and that the suit had become "practically a uniform; there is never a day, or an occasion, where I [can] resist wearing it." One such irresistible occasion had been her second day in Paris, when she gamely told reporters, "I'm enjoying this trip terribly. . . . I long to walk around and look at the buildings and the streets and sit in the cafés." This was a vain hope; her every public appearance was met with a crush of crowds. □ Jacqueline Kennedy wore the suit again to a luncheon with Nina Khrushchev at the Pallavicini Palace in Vienna, hosted by Dr. Martha Kyrle, the daughter of the Austrian president. A crowd of about three thousand people gathered in the square before the palace, chanting "Jackie," Letitia Baldrige recalled, "over and over again in bursts of rhythmic cadence." Mrs. Kennedy approached the window and waved at the crowd, then diplomatically asked Mrs. Khrushchev to join her. The two first ladies met at the open window, clasped hands, and held them aloft.

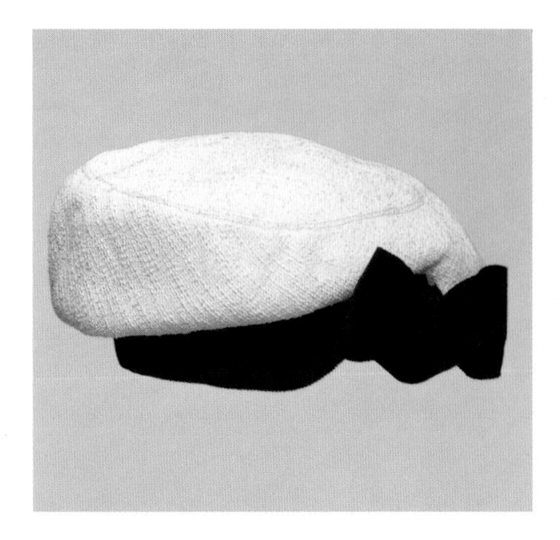

Chez Ninon, after spring–summer 1961 model number 3270 by Hubert de Givenchy. Suit in salt-and-pepper wool tweed. Museum visits with André Malraux, Paris, June 2, 1961. Address by President Kennedy to the United Nations, New York, September 21, 1961. ☐ Halston, for Bergdorf Goodman. Beret of off-white straw and nylon with black petersham ribbon, 1961. Arrival in Ottawa, May 16, 1961. Museum visits with André Malraux, Paris, June 2, 1961. ☐ In spite of the premiums that Chez Ninon paid to reproduce Paris models exactly, the house was not above making its own adaptations. Givenchy had shown this suit in an emphatic houndstooth tweed; by choosing a subtle salt-and-pepper flecked wool, Chez Ninon transformed it from a bold fashion statement into something far more understated for a client who preferred low-key effects. Jacqueline Kennedy paired it with a beret (sketch by a Bergdorf artist, above), another hat form that she was prepared to endorse; Halston gave it a playful *matelot* twist via the added structure of a grosgrain trim. ☐ The first lady wore the suit on a rainy Paris day, touring museums with André Malraux, the French minister of culture. At the Galerie Nationale du Jeu de Paume, she claimed that the painting she most admired was Manet's *Olympia* (shown below in a watercolor by Jacqueline Duhême for French *Elle* in 1961). At Malmaison, Empress Joséphine's country retreat—appointed in the pure Empire style that appealed to Mrs. Kennedy—she was struck by the humanity of the mise-en-scène, by the fresh flowers everywhere, and by a sense that the occupants had just left the house for a moment. It was an atmosphere she attempted to recapture in her restoration of the White House. Lunch was at La Celle Saint-Cloud, Madame de Pompadour's own bucolic residence. Jacqueline Kennedy had long admired Malraux, and when he kept his scheduled engagement with her despite the accidental deaths of his two sons just days earlier, she was profoundly moved. Before she left France Mrs. Kennedy wrote to him, "After all the long years I have been reading your books I never dared to hope there would be a day when I would hear—not read—your words."

Hubert de Givenchy. Evening coat in ivory silk ziberline, spring–summer 1961. Model number 3378. Dinner honoring President and Mrs. Kennedy, Palace of Versailles, June 1, 1961. Dinner for Jacqueline Kennedy hosted by Ambassador John Kenneth Galbraith, U.S. Embassy, New Delhi, India, March 20, 1962. □ With this magnificent opera coat Givenchy paid homage to Balenciaga by manipulating a great sweep of fabric (double the weight of that used for the matching dress) with a minimum of seams. Like its wearer, it managed to register as both a vision of modernity and a palimpsest of historical references, suggesting by turns a Venetian domino, a Kabuki robe, and, as General de Gaulle himself remarked to Jacqueline Kennedy, a costume in a Watteau painting.

Hubert de Givenchy. Evening dress of ivory silk ziberline embroidered by Hurel with silk floss, silk ribbon, and seed pearls, spring–summer 1961. Model number 3378. Dinner at the Palace of Versailles, June 1, 1961. Congressional reception, the White House, April 10, 1962. □ For the high point of the Kennedys' visit to France—an evening at Versailles hosted by the de Gaulles—Jacqueline Kennedy presented herself as the paradigm of French elegance. Lee Radziwill, herself a faithful Givenchy client at the time, chose this dress from the designer's collection and worked with him on subtle adaptations (the bodice had originally been darker and the embroidery bolder) to ensure that her sister's ensemble would be unique. It struck the correct note of youthful glamour. The light touch of Hurel's embroidery, with its scattered lilies of the valley and full-blown roses resembling a Louis XVI man's vest in magnified detail, suggested at once the wearer's love of flowers and her passion for the arts of eighteenth-century France. Alexandre devised a coiffure for the occasion that he called "Fontanges 1960," a reference to the hairstyle accidentally initiated by the duchesse de Fontanges, a mistress of Louis XIV, who during a hunt rearranged her disheveled hair with the aid of one of her garters, much to the king's delight. As three hundred years later a tiara might have been seen as undemocratic, Alexandre instead decorated the first lady's hair with diamond brooches borrowed from Van Cleef and Arpels. □ Thus attired, Jacqueline Kennedy joined the president in a triumphant entrance to the flourishes of forty trumpeters in full eighteenth-century regalia. Letitia Baldrige, in her spirited 1968 memoir, *Of Diamonds and Diplomats,* recalled that "a long table was set up in the Hall of Mirrors, which was lit by an incandescent glow from candles in the vermeil candelabra and by the newly illuminated frescoes in the ceiling. The entire table service was in antique vermeil, and the pinkish-golden glow cast by the candles on the surfaces was repeated in the pale peach color of the flowers down the center of the table. The women's jewels sparkled like colored fireflies on the great table—it was quite blindingly apparent that every Frenchwoman invited had borrowed the family treasures." □ After dinner the guests repaired to the exquisite theater where Louis XV had celebrated his marriage to Maria Leszczyńska for a ballet presented in the eighteenth-century manner. During the program the French president and the American first lady drew their chairs to the back of the royal box for a private talk without the aid of interpreters. Later, as the Kennedys rode through Versailles's illuminated grounds on their way back to Paris, they stopped their car and—according to Letitia Baldrige—"walked over to one of the main fountains shooting a diamond spray almost as high as the ancient trees lining the allées of the park. They just stood there in silence for a couple of minutes, hand in hand, listening to the music and savoring who knows how many precious impressions."

Oleg Cassini. Evening dress in shell pink silk-georgette chiffon embroidered with sequins, 1961. Dinner at the Schönbrunn Palace, Vienna, June 3, 1961. □ In early 1961 Eugenia Sheppard, of the New York *Herald Tribune,* had seen Nicole Alphand previewing a dress from Marc Bohan's debut collection for Dior and remarked upon its "fascinating semi-fit through the waist," which would be a theme of the collection. This detail accorded perfectly with Jacqueline Kennedy's dislike of tight clothing, and, here, Cassini incorporated it into a dress of high-voltage glamour that evoked his own Hollywood past. Emblematic of modern Western luxury and sophistication, it was a calculated choice to wear for a soiree with the Soviet premier, Nikita Khrushchev, hosted by the Austrian president, Adolf Schärf, at the Schönbrunn Palace. As the Associated Press reported on the meeting of Mrs. Kennedy and the premier for the first time, "the tough and often belligerent Communist leader looked like a smitten schoolboy when the ice thaws along the Volga in springtime." Khrushchev was visibly delighted by Jacqueline Kennedy's dazzling appearance and declared her dress "beautiful." When photographers asked him to shake hands with the president (after a day of tense and unresolved negotiations between the leaders of the two superpowers), Khrushchev replied, "I'd like to shake her hand first." □ Jacqueline Kennedy and Khrushchev maintained a spirited badinage through dinner. Mrs. Kennedy had recently read *Sabres of Paradise,* Lesley Blanch's dashing history of the Muslim tribes' resistance to Russian expansionism in the Caucasus, and attempted to engage the Soviet premier in a conversation on the subject. He responded with the comparative numbers of teachers per capita in the Soviet and Czarist Ukraine. She cut him off with the playful riposte, "Oh, Mr. Chairman, don't bore me with statistics."

Chez Ninon, after spring–summer 1961 model number 3390 by Hubert de Givenchy. Evening dress in ice blue silk shantung with matching stole, 1961. Dinner hosted by Queen Elizabeth II and Prince Philip, Buckingham Palace, London, June 5, 1961. Dinner hosted by Prime Minister Hayato Ikeda, Japanese Embassy, Washington, D.C., June 22, 1961. □ When Queen Elizabeth II and Prince Philip visited the White House in 1957 for a state dinner in their honor, Mamie Eisenhower and Great Britain's monarch had been dressed remarkably similarly. Each wore a full-skirted ball gown in pastel satin with floral motifs, shoulder straps, and swathed bodices—the preferred formal evening silhouette for the past decade. Even their close-to-the-head hairstyles and jewelry choices resembled one another's. □ Four years later, at a Buckingham Palace dinner for the Kennedys, Queen Elizabeth stayed true to her iconic state-evening look, choosing a larkspur tulle crinoline by her court dressmaker, Norman Hartnell. This time, however, America's first lady presented a startling contrast with the queen, whom she was meeting for the first time (the president had met her before the war when she was still Princess Elizabeth and his father was U.S. ambassador to the Court of St. James's). Jacqueline Kennedy, wearing Chez Ninon's freehand interpretation of a Givenchy dress, represented an image of up-to-date elegance, subliminally reinforcing the Kennedy administration's message of America's forward-thinking dynamism. The Washington *Post* noted that "the First Lady silently and smilingly stole the show. . . . her popularity rating here is just as high as it was in Paris or Vienna."

Hubert de Givenchy. Dress and jacket of deep pink wool bouclé with passementerie button, spring–summer 1959. Model number 2460. Luncheon with Queen Elizabeth II, Buckingham Palace, London, March 28, 1962. Visit to Junior Village, an institution for homeless children, Washington, D.C., December 13, 1962. □ This prophetic 1959 Givenchy ensemble illustrates several sartorial details that would become staples of Jacqueline Kennedy's state clothing: the sleeveless dress, with a degree of practical fullness concealed in its apparently narrow skirt, and the boxy jacket, with its three-quarter-length sleeves and overscaled button trim (here used as a single design accent to offset the squareness of the jacket). Mrs. Kennedy wore this dress and jacket from her pre–White House wardrobe for a luncheon with Queen Elizabeth at Buckingham Palace, in the wake of her India and Pakistan tour. "I'm feeling full of beans and very excited about having lunch with the Queen," Mrs. Kennedy confided to the press corps. She later revealed that they had compared notes on India and Pakistan and discussed their mutual interest in horses and riding.

Oleg Cassini. Dress in black silk-and-wool Alaskine, 1962. Audience with Pope John XXIII, the Vatican, March 11, 1962. □ Jacqueline Kennedy and Oleg Cassini revealed their shared sense of theater in the dress designed for the first lady's audience with Pope John XXIII. In its ascetic magnificence the dress has the stately presence of a seventeenth-century Spanish portrait (to enhance the pictorial effect, a trapezoidal taffeta farthingale petticoat supports the weight of the skirts). Required to wear a head covering, Mrs. Kennedy draped a dramatic black mantilla over an elaborate Spanish comb. Dismissing interpreters, she and the pontiff conversed in French in his library for an unusually long private audience before exchanging gifts. She presented him with an inscribed copy of the president's collected speeches and a velvet-lined vermeil box that she had commissioned. He, in turn, gave her a rosary and a set of papal medals for her children.

Oleg Cassini. Coat in bright pink silk-and-wool Alaskine, 1962. Arrival in New Delhi, March 12, 1962. ☐ Halston, for Bergdorf Goodman. Hat in hot pink straw with grosgrain ribbon, 1962. Model number 4536. Arrival in New Delhi, March 12, 1962. ☐ Bergdorf Goodman. Hat of natural parabuntal straw, 1962. Model number 4536-1. Placing flowers at Mahatma Gandhi's shrine, New Delhi, March 12, 1962. ☐ Jacqueline Kennedy's wardrobe for her trip to India and Pakistan was a triumph of iconography. She established a palette appropriately inspired by Mughal miniatures and interspersed with ivory, a color that set her apart from the backdrop of vivid saris. This pattern of complementary clothing was set on arrival at New Delhi's airport (above), where she was greeted by Prime Minister Jawaharlal Nehru and his daughter, Indira Gandhi. She wore a pink hat and a fashionable abstraction of a rajah coat (a form that Nehru himself endorsed) in a color that John Kenneth Galbraith, the U.S. ambassador to India, memorably described as "radioactive pink." ☐ Afterward, Mrs. Kennedy changed into an ivory version of the hot pink coat, with which she wore a straw cartwheel hat. In this more subdued outfit she began her official schedule, calling on the country's seventy-seven-year-old President Rajendra Prasad at the Rashtrapati Bhavan, his residence (below). She later visited the shore of the Jumna River, where she laid white roses on the shrine of Mahatma Gandhi. "For a Caucasian woman to show such a respect to a third world people was rare," as Carl Sferrazza Anthony noted (in *First Ladies,* published in 1991), "and it won her unanimous praise in India."

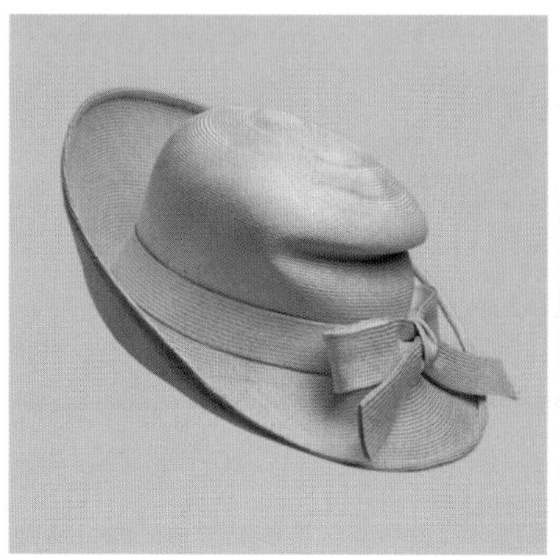

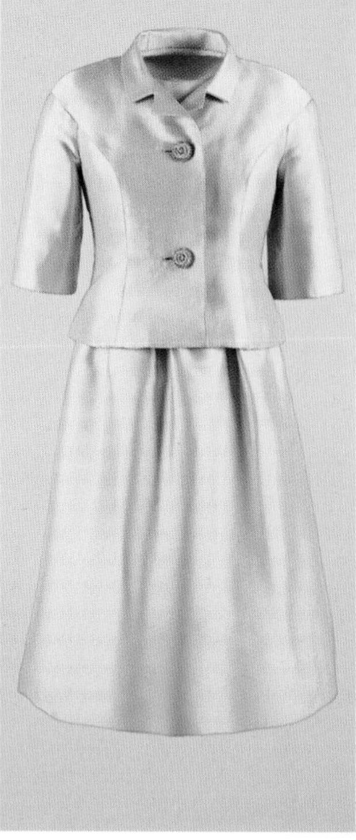

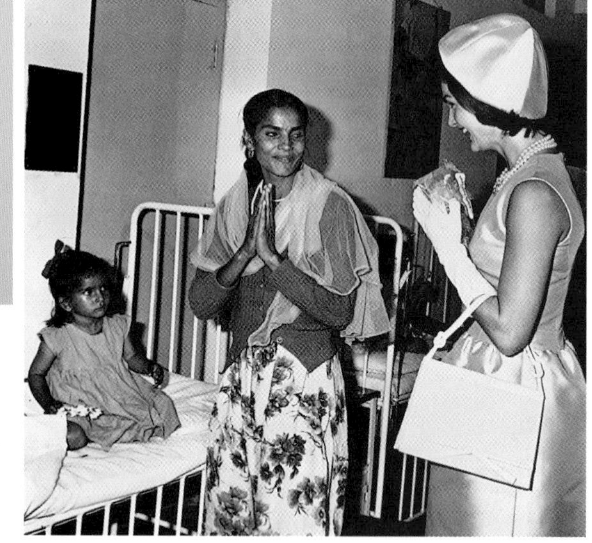

Gustave Tassell (American, born 1926). Dress and jacket in ice blue silk ziberline with passementerie buttons, 1962. Visit to the All-India Institute of Medical Sciences and tour of the gardens at the prime minister's residence, New Delhi, March 13, 1962. □ Bergdorf Goodman. Beret of ice blue silk ziberline, 1962. Model number 311-3. □ Gustave Tassell's clothes, *Holiday* magazine stated in June 1962, "demand a great deal from the wearer—mainly a built-in serenity of the kind that emanates so effortlessly from the first lady and Princesses Rainier and Radziwill." For this ensemble Tassell derived inspiration from a 1961 Balenciaga model—a Joe Eula sketch appeared in the New York *Times*'s Paris collections report of spring 1961—and converted it from a suit to a dress and jacket. The gathers of the low-set skirt, the three-quarter-length sleeves (designed to be filled in with gloves or draw attention to bracelets), and the high indentation of the jacket's waist are Balenciaga trademarks taken up by many of his contemporaries. Tassell's focus on fine workmanship and fabrics—and his injunction to "forget fashion. You can't go around startling people all the time"—would have attracted Mrs. Kennedy. □ The beret was a favorite of Mrs. Kennedy's. The unusual sectional form of this example suggests the geometric approach that Halston would take in his debut as a clothing designer at Bergdorf's in 1967. □ Jacqueline Kennedy wore the dress without the jacket on her second day in India, when she spent the morning with young patients at the All-India Institute of Medical Sciences and the afternoon with Jawaharlal Nehru touring the gardens of the prime minister's residence. Nehru, a skilled leader in India's struggle for independence, became India's first prime minister in 1948 and was greatly admired by the president and first lady. The U.S. ambassador, John Kenneth Galbraith, noted afterward that Mrs. Kennedy's trip had helped Indian-American relations.

Oleg Cassini. Dress and coat in apricot silk ziberline, 1962. Lake Pichola cruise, Udaipur, March 17, 1962. □ For her daytime boat ride on Lake Pichola, Jacqueline Kennedy wore a dress and a coat of such elegant formality that they would not have been out of place at a fashionable cocktail party on Fifth Avenue. However, this Cassini ensemble brilliantly served Mrs. Kennedy's needs: the fabric was rigid enough to keep its composure in the heat of India, and its dazzling color (appropriate to the intended setting) and sheen were calculated to ensure that she would be instantly identifiable to the crowds on the distant shore as they watched her boat on its way to the maharana of Udaipur's white palace, where she was feted that evening.

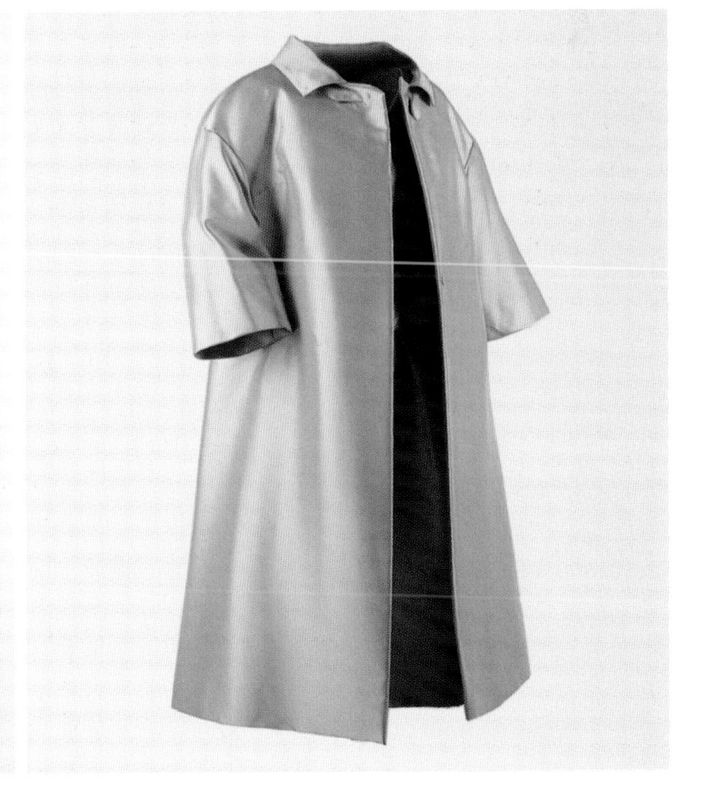

Gustave Tassell. Dress in pale yellow silk ziberline with matching stole, 1962. Jaipur, March 19, 1962. □ During a two-day holiday as the guests of the maharaja and maharani of Jaipur, Jacqueline Kennedy met with members of the Peace Corps and was later joined by her sister for an elephant ride on the grounds of the Amber Palace. □ In private life Mrs. Kennedy endorsed slacks but for her state clothing maintained a high degree of formality. Even with the prospect of an elephant ride, Jacqueline Kennedy and her sister wore rather fanciful short dresses and pumps. Although Mrs. Kennedy's Tassell dress had an uncharacteristically ballooning skirt to ensure some level of mobility, her outfit was far from the safari suit that Queen Elizabeth had worn to ride the same elephant on her visit the year before. □ With Mrs. Kennedy's wardrobe in mind, Indian officials had constructed an elaborately decorated platform so that she and Princess Radziwill could mount the flamboyantly painted pachyderm, Bibia, with the appropriate degree of dignity. □ The first lady is shown at top right with U.S. ambassador John Kenneth Galbraith.

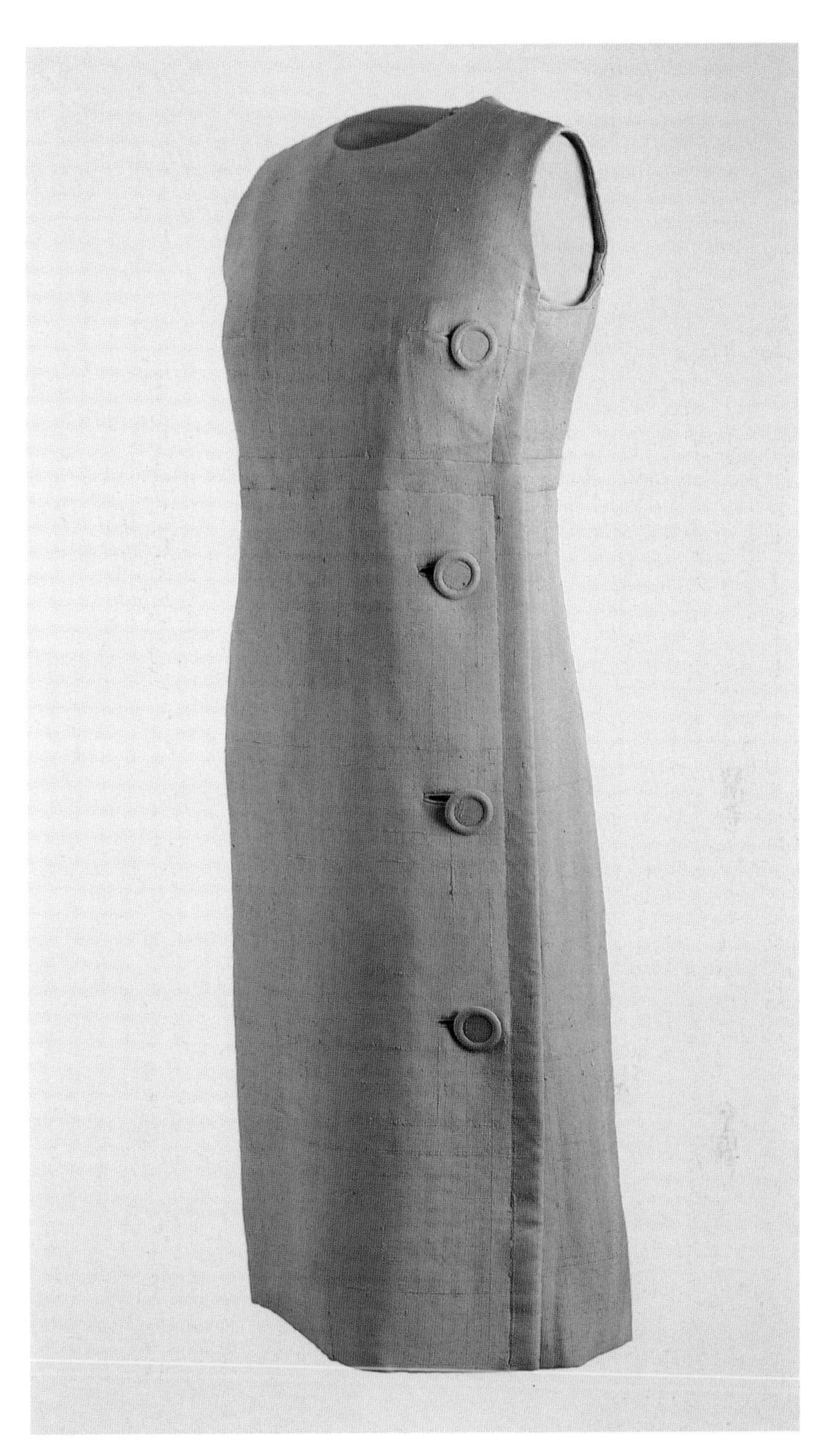

Donald Brooks (American, born 1928), for Townley (American, established 1948). Empire-waisted shift in hot pink silk shantung, 1962. Cruise on the Ganges River, Benares, March 16, 1962. □ Jacqueline Kennedy acquired her Townley clothes through Dorcas Harden, a stylish Georgetown hostess whose discreet Washington boutique had been a favorite resource for a decade. In their unstructured ease, Brooks's fashions continued the legacy of Townley's original designer, Claire McCardell (who had died in 1958). For Mrs. Kennedy, they were useful supplements to the formality of her state wardrobe and ideal for such situations as her March 1962 cruise on the Ganges. □ "On that hot morning," remembered Jacqueline Duhême, an artist and a protégée of Henri Matisse who accompanied Mrs. Kennedy to India and Pakistan and wrote of this experience in *Mrs. Kennedy Goes Abroad* (1998), "Jacqueline appeared hatless and stockingless in a shocking-pink dress that complemented the jewel tones of India. She boarded a boat garlanded with marigolds to view the bathing spots and cremation platforms along the riverside. Scarlet-liveried bearers sheltered Jacqueline and Lee with parasols as large crowds along the banks blew deafening blasts on conch shells and banged on triangles in excitement and appreciation. Later, Jacqueline walked up a petal-strewn path to Sarnath Stupa, the temple from which Buddha preached his first sermon two thousand five hundred years ago."

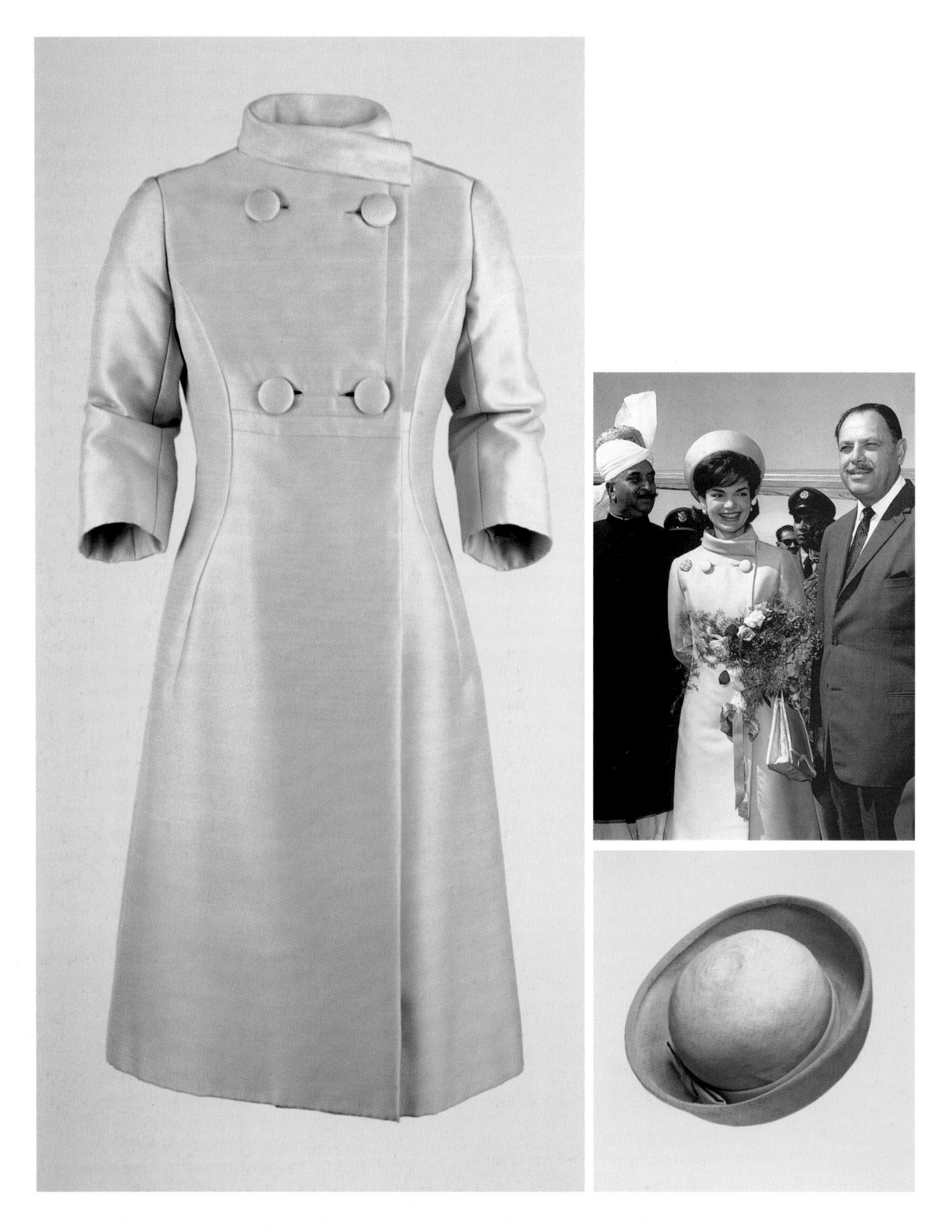

Oleg Cassini. Coat in pale blue silk-and-wool Alaskine, 1962. Arrival in Lahore, March 21, 1962. □ Bergdorf Goodman. Hat of pale blue baku straw, 1962. Model number 4537. □ The seaming on this coat suggests an hourglass—a dress form to which Cassini was particularly attached—although here it is subordinated to Jacqueline Kennedy's own preference for clothing that implies but does not define the body beneath. In Lahore, the New York *Journal-American* wrote, she was greeted "with a carnival-like reception that brought out [President Mohammad Ayub Khan]" (above right) along with "thousands of school children."

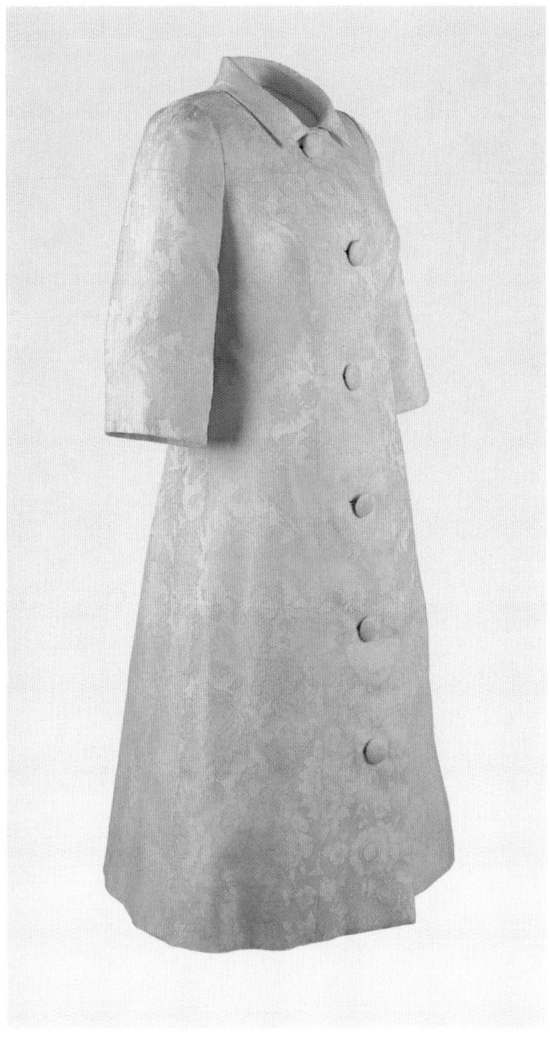

Gustave Tassell. Single-breasted A-line coat in acid yellow silk jacquard, 1962. Visit to the Shalimar Gardens, Lahore, March 22, 1962. □ Tassell relied on the subtle luxury of fabric for effect—here, a fragile silk jacquard that manages to suggest an opulent brocade. The first lady wore the coat for an evening that began with a fashion show modeled by society girls from Lahore in costumes representing the history of Pakistan and its mythology. Two of the models in nylon saris drew laughs from the audience because of their "Jackie hairdos." □ Later, Jacqueline Kennedy visited the seventeenth-century Shalimar Gardens, built by Shāh Jahān as a tribute to his father. Designed in magnificent Mughal style, the gardens are terraced and have three reflecting pools with more than four hundred fountains and numerous marble pavilions. President Mohammad Ayub Khan presented her with a scale model in elaborately chased silver (right), and she told the seven thousand invited guests that "all my life I have dreamed of coming to Shalimar and never thought it would happen. It is even lovelier than I had imagined." She added that she was "profoundly impressed by the reverence which you in Pakistan have for your art and for your culture."

Gustave Tassell. Dress and coat in scarlet, orange, and hot pink printed and ribbed silk matelassé, 1962. Arrival in Rajasthan, March 18, 1962. Camel ride, Karachi, March 25, 1962. □ For her state clothing Jacqueline Kennedy generally avoided prints, preferring the impact of strong solid colors. In this rare example she chose a pointillist pattern that, seen from afar, blends into an even more intense hue than a solid color could be expected to achieve—an ideal choice for the first lady in the flamboyantly dressed throng that greeted her in Rajasthan. □ She also wore the dress on its own for a camel ride with her sister on the grounds of President Mohammad Ayub Khan's residence in Karachi. Their camel driver was Bashir Ahmed, who had met Lyndon Johnson on the vice president's earlier trip to Pakistan and had surprised officials by taking Johnson up on an invitation to visit him at the White House. Because of their skirts both women had to sit sidesaddle, making their ride even more unsteady. Lee Radziwill lost a shoe in the process. Their ride is depicted at top right in a watercolor by Jacqueline Duhême for *McCall's* magazine in 1962.

Norman Norell (American, 1900–1972). Dress in denim-blue linen, 1960. Visit to the Parthenon, Athens, June 11, 1961. □ Norman Norell was one of a triumvirate of designers whom Diana Vreeland recommended to Jacqueline Kennedy for her wardrobe needs as first lady (the others were Stella Sloat and Ben Zuckerman) before Oleg Cassini was chosen. Norell was America's preeminent ready-to-wear designer at the time, renowned for his luxurious understatements and his breezy American revisions of European couture. This dress reveals Norell's twin allegiances: its sophisticated simplicity shows the influence of Paris on the designer's work, while the fabric suggests that quintessentially American material—denim. After the Kennedys' 1961 European tour the president returned to Washington, while Mrs. Kennedy and her sister traveled to Greece for a week's vacation. During their stay they lunched with the Greek royal family, cruised the islands, and toured the Parthenon.

Colombia

Gustave Tassell. Coat in pistachio green wool bouclé, 1961. Arrival in Bogotá, December 17, 1961. □ Halston, for Bergdorf Goodman. Hat in pale pistachio green stitched silk, 1961. Model number 4231. □ The quiet luxury of Tassell's clothing is exemplified by this elegant coat. Its lean lines and restraining buttons made it an appropriate choice for the arrival ceremonies at Bogotá's airport (where Mrs. Kennedy stood at attention and listened to welcoming speeches), but it would not do for her tour of a children's hospital later that day. For that visit, she needed an outfit that would allow for greater mobility and so changed into a Cassini suit (right), illustrating just how thorough her wardrobe planning could be. Unusually, the first lady's press office named Gustave Tassell as the designer of this coat; it did not normally publicize this information, leaving the popular press to infer (as was generally the case) that a given garment had been designed by Oleg Cassini. Mrs. Kennedy wore several more Tassell pieces on her tour of India and Pakistan the following year, but the nonfashion press generally attributed these to Cassini. □ Colombia was the last stop on the Kennedys' triumphant 6,300-mile South American tour. In Bogotá Mrs. Kennedy and the president were welcomed by President Alberto Lleras Camargo and, as the Associated Press's Frances Lewine reported, "half a million or more cheering, flag-waving enthusiastic Colombians . . . showered them with confetti and flower petals."

Oleg Cassini. Day suit in pale yellow wool, 1961. Ottawa, May 17, 1961. Visit to a children's hospital, Bogotá, December 17, 1961. □ Bergdorf Goodman, after Jean Barthet (French, born 1930). Hat in pale yellow woven straw with silk gardenia, 1961. Model number 4216. □ This archetypal Cassini suit, with the designer's trademark self-fabric buttons and crisply defined dressmaker details, belies its apparent two-dimensionality. The short-waisted jacket was deliberately cut longer in back so that it would maintain its composure if the wearer had to stoop or to wave. Jacqueline Kennedy wore this suit to visit a children's hospital in Bogotá, where she bent down to talk with a sick child.

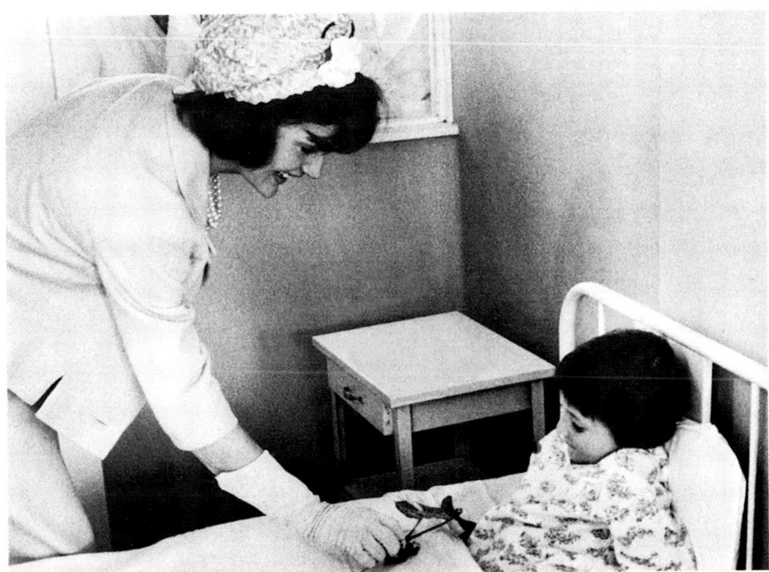

Venezuela

Marc Bohan, for Christian Dior. Dress and coat ("Vie en Rose") in apricot linen, spring–summer 1961. Luncheon with the Greek royal family, Athens, June 13, 1961. Address to farmers about the Alliance for Progress initiative, La Morita Resettlement Project, near Caracas, December 16, 1961. □ After the debacle of Yves Saint Laurent's radical but unpopular "beatnik" collection (fall–winter 1960) for Dior, the house appointed Marc Bohan, of Christian Dior–London, to replace him. Bohan had trained with Robert Piguet, known for the reticent elegance of his clothes, and then established a name for himself as the designer at Jean Patou. His debut collection for Dior was "the *succès fou* of Paris," *Vogue* breathlessly reported. "Back again was the old Dior tradition of desirable, wearable clothes." □ Bohan-inspired elements, like the dropped, unfitted waist and the soft movement of pleated skirts, swiftly found their way into Jacqueline Kennedy's wardrobe. This ensemble, however, was a Christian Dior original. Bohan had shown it in pink and named it "Vie en Rose"; Jacqueline Kennedy's version was made in apricot. Although the incriminating Paris label was carefully removed from the coat (but not from the dress), the deft workmanship betrays the hand of the Dior ateliers. □ President Kennedy sought new relations with Latin American countries through his Alliance for Progress program. He aspired to make the United States a partner in the social and economic development in the region instead of an exploiter of its resources. On state visits to Central and South America he toured the locations where the work of the Alliance was taking place. Jacqueline Kennedy's fluency in Spanish was a tremendous asset. At La Morita, Venezuela, during a ceremony to present land titles to eighty-six families, the president introduced his wife as "one of the Kennedys who does not need an interpreter." The first lady then delivered her own remarks in Spanish to resounding applause.

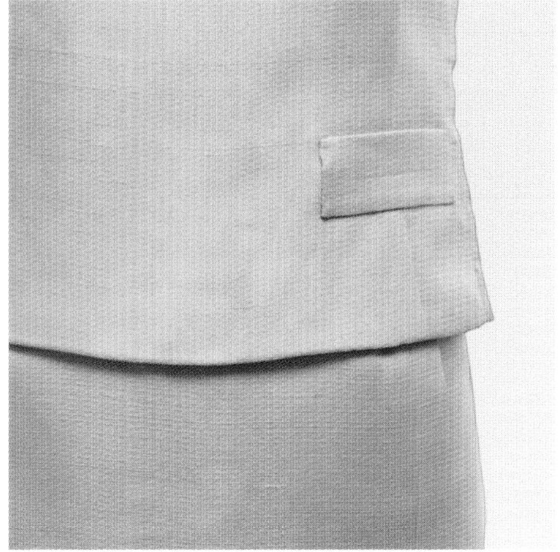

Oleg Cassini. Day ensemble of shell, skirt, and coat in leaf green silk gazar, with matching hat, 1962. Arrival in Mexico City, June 29, 1962. □ This ensemble is a classic example of Jacqueline Kennedy's collaboration with Cassini and his studios. The lines of the coat were derived from an example by Jacques Heim that appeared in an advertisement in the March 1962 issue of the French fashion magazine *L'Art et la mode,* and the sleeveless bodice, with its off-center horizontal pocket detail, is similar to the spring–summer 1961 Christian Dior original in Mrs. Kennedy's own collection (p. 158). Cassini abstracted and exaggerated the lines of these pieces, however, investing them with a completely new dimension through different fabric and color. The first lady wore the ensemble when she and the president disembarked from Air Force One at Mexico City's airport. Twenty-one guns saluted as President Adolfo López Mateos and his wife (joined by a crowd of twenty-five thousand shouting "Arriba Kennedy! Arriba Jacquelina!") welcomed them to the country where they had honeymooned almost nine years earlier. The tarmac featured a vast floral depiction of Presidents Kennedy and López Mateos shaking hands. From the airport the motorcade moved slowly to the presidential residence along a ten-mile parade route lined by one-and-a-half million people—almost a third of Mexico City's population. "For the President and his wife," wrote *Life,* "it was a second, and very public honeymoon with the Mexican people."

Oleg Cassini. Evening dress in azure blue silk crepe Giselle, 1962. Foreign ministry reception, Mexico City, June 29, 1962. Dinner hosted by Ambassador Howard Beale, the Breakers, Newport, Rhode Island, September 14, 1962. ☐ The inspiration for this dress was an illustration by Fanny Darnat of a Givenchy model that appeared in *Femme Chic*'s summer 1962 issue, where it was shown with its original white daisy-lace bolero. Cassini took this reference merely as a starting point, however, producing a dress in striking azure blue crepe—part of his coherent color statement for the Mexico tour (below)—that bears the quintessential imprimatur of his client. ☐ Jacqueline Kennedy wore it three months after the Mexico trip for a dinner in Newport during America's Cup week (above). Sir Howard Beale, Australia's ambassador to the United States, gave the dinner in the Kennedys' honor at the Breakers, the Vanderbilts' celebrated summer "cottage." In deference to this opulent Belle Epoque setting, Kenneth gave the first lady a "Gibson Girl" upswept hairstyle. Despite this touch, and the antique diamond starburst pinned to the dress's bow (as it had been in Mexico), Jacqueline Kennedy appeared resolutely contemporary. The New York *Times*'s Carrie Donovan reported that "in general, the women wore traditional, sedate ball gowns," but that Mrs. Kennedy provided "a definite contrast to the conservative element. She looked like a beautiful movie star." In his after-dinner remarks Ambassador Beale praised the first lady, saying she had brought to her position "personal qualities of character and charm which make it natural and inevitable that she should be regarded with the highest respect and honor, not only by us here tonight, but by her countrymen everywhere."

Oleg Cassini, after Karl Lagerfeld for Jean Patou. Top and skirt in hot pink silk shantung, 1962. Luncheon with President Adolfo López Mateos at the María Isabel Hotel, Mexico City, June 30, 1962. Bergdorf Goodman. Hat of hot pink parabuntal straw, 1962. Model number 4842. □ Jacqueline Kennedy scoured American, French, and English fashion magazines for ideas that could be reworked into her own wardrobe. Here, she and Cassini dramatically reinterpreted a suit originally designed by Karl Lagerfeld for Jean Patou and photographed for the French magazine *L'Officiel* in March 1962. Like that of several other French magazines to which she subscribed (including *L'Art et la mode*), *L'Officiel*'s approach to fashion photography was documentary rather than fanciful, making it a boon for copyists and the "little dressmakers" on whom many women with pretensions to fashionable elegance then relied. These magazines also published precise details of the fabrics and of the houses that made them. In this instance, however, Mrs. Kennedy and Cassini followed only the crisp geometry of line that would remain a leitmotif in Lagerfeld's work. Lagerfeld's original was designed in a thick orange tweed, but in a light shantung, suitable for Mexico's summer heat, the suit was transformed. □ The evening before the luncheon, President Adolfo López Mateos had presented the first lady with a box of gold jewelry of Mayan inspiration, and from this she diplomatically chose a necklace to wear with her outfit. At the luncheon she again charmed her audience with a speech in Spanish.

Oleg Cassini, after spring–summer 1962 model by Jules-François Crahay, for Nina Ricci. Day suit in pale yellow linen, 1962. Visit to the National Institute for the Protection of Children, Mexico City, June 30, 1962. □ Bergdorf Goodman. Hat of natural straw with black grosgrain ribbon, 1962. Model number 4387. □ Nina Ricci's Jules-François Crahay was popular with young-minded couture clients (including President Kennedy's sisters) and the fashion press for his breezy design statements. The lines of this Cassini suit were adapted from one that Crahay showed in his spring–summer 1962 couture collection. Ricci's American licensee, Mademoiselle Ricci, also adapted it for a ready-to-wear version, a photograph of which appeared in *Vogue*'s April 15, 1962, issue. Cassini revised it in uncrushable linen, appropriate for a Mexico City summer, and in one of the "sun colors" that he and Mrs. Kennedy had selected for her wardrobe on this state visit. The crisp finishing touch of a dressmaker bow is found on many of Jacqueline Kennedy's state evening clothes. She wore this suit on her second afternoon in Mexico, when she toured the National Institute for the Protection of Children, a school lunch factory sponsored by Mexico's first lady, Eva Sámano de López Mateos. Mrs. Kennedy handed out lollipops and giant rag dolls and pinned PT 109 tie clips (a symbol of the president's World War II naval exploits on a patrol torpedo boat and his Oval Office giveaway of choice) on the shirts of the young boys.

Joan Morse, for A La Carte. Day dress in rose pink honeycomb-weave wool, 1962. Addressing members of Brigade 2506, Miami, December 29, 1962. Visiting the amphitheater at Delphi, Greece, October 1963. □ Acquired from Joan Morse's Manhattan boutique, this dress bears many of the classic Jacqueline Kennedy hallmarks—an overblouse effect, a modified A-line flare to the skirt, a sleeveless shell bodice, a crisp bow—thus illustrating that these iconic elements had been absorbed by designers working at every level. Mrs. Kennedy wore it in Miami to greet members of Brigade 2506, Cuban exiles who had participated in the failed Bay of Pigs invasion on April 17, 1961, and been imprisoned by the Castro regime for their defiance. Months of negotiations with the U.S. Department of Justice finally secured their release. After assuring the exiles of America's commitment to a free and democratic Cuba, President Kennedy asked his wife to address them in their native language: "It is an honor for me to be here today with a group of the bravest men in the world. . . . I feel proud that my son has known the officers. He is still too young to realize what has happened here, but I will make it my business to tell him the story of your courage as he grows up. It is my wish and my hope that some day he may be a man at least half as brave as the members of Brigade 2506. Good luck."

Herbert Sondheim (American, 1895–1966). Day dress in turquoise silk shantung, ca. 1960. Richard Avedon photographic sitting with Caroline Kennedy, Palm Beach, Florida, January 5, 1961. Good Friday service, Saint Edward's Church, Palm Beach, April 20, 1962. □ While Jacqueline Kennedy's "state clothes" were uniforms that reflected the dignity of her role, in her off-duty moments she dressed with insouciant modernity. For a Good Friday service in Palm Beach she galvanized America by eschewing the hidebound, formalized elegance of the fifties that decreed hats and cover-up for church. Instead, she wore a favorite sleeveless sundress by the popular Seventh Avenue manufacturer Herbert Sondheim (father of the songwriter Stephen), who was known for the ladylike propriety of his clothes. In a head scarf, goggle-eyed, white-framed sunglasses, and Jack Rogers sandals, she was dressed much like any other young Palm Beach *élégante,* but much of America thought otherwise. "Little did we realize that we would have . . . in Jackie, a sort of beatnik—a gilded one of course," wrote one outraged citizen. □ The head scarf was already a fashionable accoutrement in Jacqueline Kennedy's circle; her friend Dorinda Dixon Ryan (a youthful fixture on the Best Dressed list, whose idiosyncratic fashion tastes bore the imprimatur of Diana Vreeland, with whom she worked as a fashion editor at *Harper's Bazaar*), for instance, had worn Norell's chin-tied scarf as a wedding veil for her 1954 marriage to John Barry Ryan III. In an era of time-consuming hairdressing statements, the instant cover-up of a scarf was a modern, logical solution. The New York *Times* later reported that "the practical kerchief has suddenly become the *dernier cri* in fashion. It may have all started last spring when Mrs. John F. Kennedy was photographed leaving church with a babushka covering her coiffure." Her endorsement even impacted Paris couture. For their spring and fall 1962 shows, both Yves Saint Laurent and Karl Lagerfeld at Jean Patou showed head scarves in place of hats with their thoroughly contemporary collections.

Oleg Cassini. Day dress in pale mauve linen, 1963. Easter Sunday, Palm Beach, Florida, April 14, 1963. □ In addition to the formal clothing that Oleg Cassini produced for the first lady, he also provided her with casual items, such as pastel sundresses for her Palm Beach wardrobe. In this characteristic example Cassini qualified the garment's absolutely modern simplicity of form with a token element of decoration—a quatrefoil motif, perhaps an abstraction of a cockade, applied to the front of the dress. Jacqueline Kennedy wore it to a private Easter mass at the Palm Beach home of the president's parents, Ambassador and Mrs. Joseph P. Kennedy. Perhaps in response to the furor that had attended her casual appearance for the Good Friday service in Palm Beach at Saint Edward's Church the year before (p. 170), this time she countered the understated lines of the dress with formal accessories: white kid gloves and a pale lace mantilla.

Renauld of France. Sunglasses, ca. 1962. Ravello, August 1962. □ Sunglasses had been part of Jacqueline Bouvier's casual wardrobe as early as her trip to Europe with her sister in 1951. In her off-duty moments as first lady, they served a purpose both practical and protective, as she later revealed in conversation with André Previn. When the celebrated conductor asked whether she was disturbed by the public's relentless scrutiny, she replied, "That's why I always wear my dark glasses. It may be that they're looking at me, but none of them can ever tell which ones I'm looking back at. That way I can have fun with it!" □ Jacqueline Kennedy wore this futuristic pair on a private trip to Ravello in the summer of 1962. There, on Italy's Amalfi coast, she revealed her thoroughly modern tastes, wearing Pucci swimsuits and backless sundresses and dancing the twist and the cha-cha in the glamorous company of Marella Agnelli, the supremely elegant wife of the Fiat magnate (in stripes, overleaf), and the designer Princess Irene Galitzine.

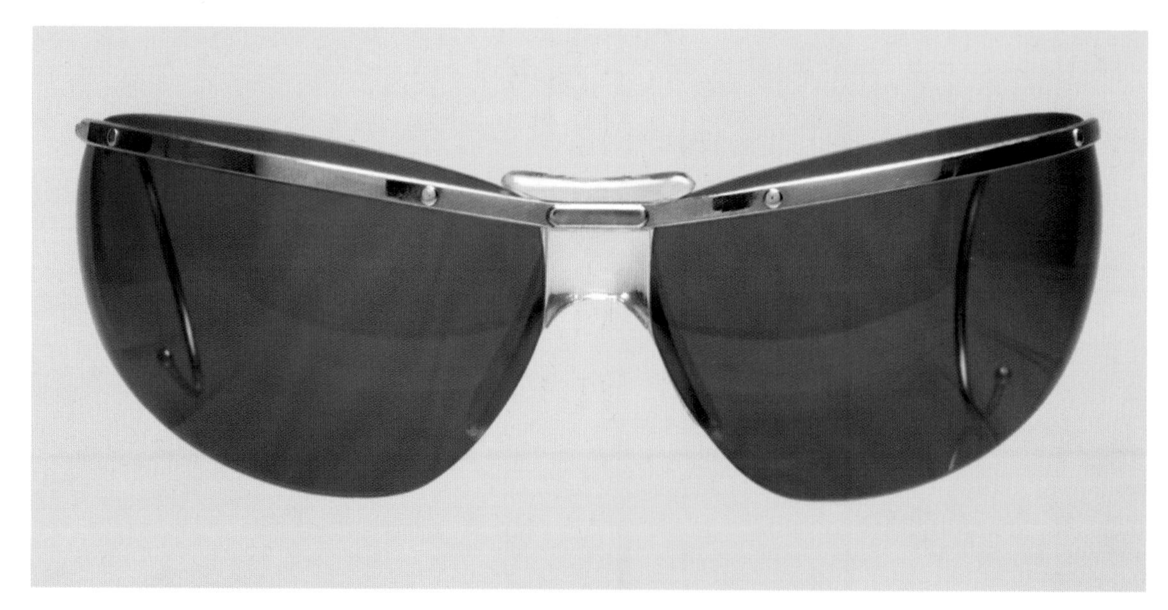

Hats

Oh dear it was so pleasant when I didn't have to wear hats!" wrote Jacqueline Kennedy to Marita O'Connor, her saleswoman in Bergdorf Goodman's millinery department, in mid-November 1960. Her natural dislike of hats was so great that even on her wedding day, when a hat would have been de rigueur for the going-away outfit, she carried, but did not wear, an emerald velvet creation that she considered unflattering. As a politician's wife, however, she was required to make concessions in this area. At the time there were situations in which a bare head might have been construed as disrespectful, and the powerful milliners' union, under the leadership of Alex Rose—who also had to contend with John F. Kennedy's reluctance to wear hats—lobbied to persuade her to support the industry.

As a result, Jacqueline Kennedy was compelled to acquire some hats for her wardrobe and sought out such respected purveyors as Lilly Daché (at whose beauty emporium her hairdresser, Kenneth Battelle, worked), the flamboyant Mr. John, and Emme salon (for which Adolfo designed). By the fall of 1960, however, she had turned to Bergdorf's almost exclusively for her millinery needs. The prestigious hat department was run by a formidable saleswoman, Jessica Daube, known, in the standard fashion parlance of the time, by the formal title of Miss Jessica. As one of the younger clients, Jacqueline Kennedy worked with O'Connor, one of Miss Jessica's junior saleswomen. The in-house custom hat designer was Roy Halston Frowick, who had apprenticed with Lilly Daché before joining Bergdorf's in 1959. Halston accompanied Ethel Frankau on her couture-buying trips to Paris and acquired hats and hat blocks from the preeminent couture houses, including Dior, Saint Laurent, Givenchy, and Balenciaga. Mrs. Kennedy ordered reinterpretations of these Paris models (and copies after such Paris milliners as Jean Barthet), as well as original models designed by Halston himself.

Halston and Jacqueline Kennedy shared the same hat size, and according to Tom Fallon, Halston's assistant at Bergdorf's in 1967 (when he launched his fashion line), he "would put her hats on his head and sit there and look at them with two mirrors, one behind him [and] one in front, turning his head at different angles to make sure they looked right." Occasionally, Jacqueline Kennedy visited Halston in his Bergdorf's salon, and if her appointment followed one with her hairdresser, in order to preserve her coif she would sit for Halston's sketch artist, Audrey Schilt, instead of trying on the hats. To keep her hats firmly in place without crushing her bouffant hairstyle, they were often secured with two or three hat pins (their heads covered in the same fabric as the hat) or with plastic-tortoiseshell combs sewn on each side of the grosgrain ribbon that defined the interior circumference of the crown. (One of Halston's best-selling items at Bergdorf's was a thick, padded hair band designed to protect his clients' voluminous hairstyles underneath their head scarves.) Although primarily associated with the iconic pillbox shape, Mrs. Kennedy would later experiment with deep cloche hat crowns, also perched high on her head, in contrast to the original 1920s skull-tight cloche. For her visits to hot climates she ordered hats with broad brims, which swept away from her face. Jacqueline Kennedy understood that the public demanded instant visibility from her, not mystery, and her hats were always selected with this purpose in mind.

Halston, for Bergdorf Goodman. Pillbox hat of fawn felt, early 1960s. Model number 2784. □ Halston, for Bergdorf Goodman. Pillbox hat of black leather, 1960. Model number F900-5. □ At the end of 1960, having established with Bergdorf Goodman's custom hat department that the pillbox shape met her millinery needs, Jacqueline Kennedy ordered several variants—here sketched by Halston's artists—of her white felt Givenchy pillbox, including examples shown here in black leather and fawn-colored felt.

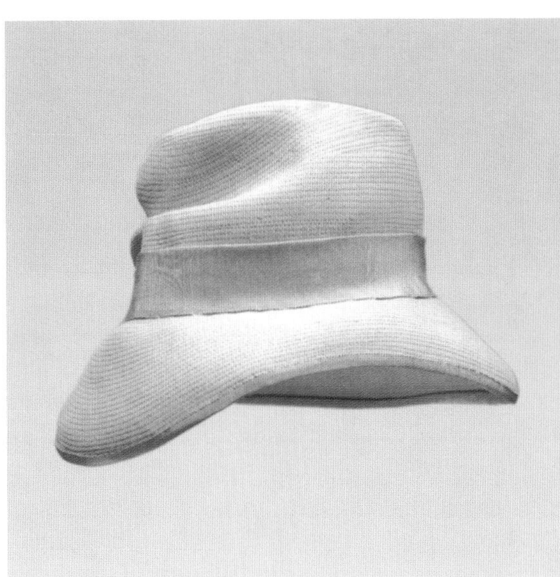

Jean Barthet. Cloche in beige felt with grosgrain ribbon, 1961. Heathrow Airport, London, June 4, 1961. □ Halston, for Bergdorf Goodman. Beret in navy wool knit with grosgrain ribbon, 1961. Model number 3343-1. Welcoming ceremony for President Manuel Prado of Peru, Washington, D.C., September 19, 1961. □ It was the Parisian hairstylist Alexandre who suggested that Jean Barthet, then the darling of the Paris millinery scene, make a hat for Jacqueline Kennedy. She had ordered Barthet adaptations through Bergdorf's before, but this cloche, worn for her arrival in London from Vienna, was a dramatic and newsworthy departure from her traditional off-the-face style. To create and define its elaborate contours, Barthet's skilled technicians used finely spaced rows of machine stitching. □ Halston gave structure to the traditionally soft beret form in the stiffly lined example below.

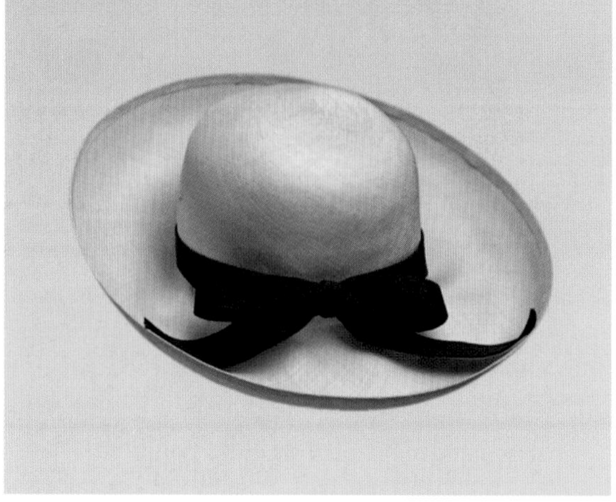

Bergdorf Goodman. Breton hat in natural straw with navy grosgrain ribbon, 1962. Model number 4536-1. □ Welcoming ceremony for Mohammad Reza Shah Pahlavi and Shabanou Farah Diba, the shah and empress of Iran, National Airport, Washington, D.C., April 11, 1962. □ Jacqueline Kennedy dressed with studied understatement—in a simple navy suit, with a straw Breton hat and Christian Dior handbag—to greet the shah and his fashionable wife. At the state dinner for the imperial couple that evening, the empress appeared as the glittering embodiment of the Peacock Throne in a gold lamé ball gown by Marc Bohan for Dior, thickly embroidered with jewels, and an astonishing parure—crown, necklace, bracelet, earrings, and brooch—of emeralds and diamonds. Against this crowded magnificence, Mrs. Kennedy's simpler effects stood out dramatically.

Bergdorf Goodman. Hat in navy lacquered straw with navy silk satin ribbon, 1963. Model number 5678. Welcoming ceremony for King Hassan II of Morocco, Union Station, Washington, D.C., March 27, 1963. □ Bergdorf Goodman. Hat in chartreuse silk shantung, 1962. Model number 4692. Launching of the nuclear submarine USS *Lafayette,* Groton, Connecticut, May 8, 1962. □ Jacqueline Kennedy wore a modified variant of Barthet's face-framing cloche to greet King Hassan II of Morocco at Washington's Union Station (above). Later that evening the first couple honored him with a White House state dinner, at which he and Mrs. Kennedy established a cordial rapport, based in part on their shared interest in horses. Six months later Jacqueline Kennedy and her sister were the king's personal guests in Marrakech, where the entertainments were, Lee Radziwill recalls, "straight out of the *Arabian Nights.*" □ At the launching of the submarine, named for the French diplomat and soldier who served under George Washington in the Revolutionary War, Jacqueline Kennedy offered brief remarks in two languages, then winced as she shattered a bottle against the hull.

Riding

Janet Lee Bouvier was an accomplished equestrienne who passed her skill and passion on to her older daughter. Jacqueline Bouvier began riding at the age of three and trained in the riding ring at Lasata, her paternal grandparents' house on Further Lane in East Hampton. By five she was striving for blue ribbons in the East End horse shows—and often winning them. In 1937, for instance, she won the under-nine equitation class at the prestigious horse show in Southampton; in 1940, at age eleven, she won every event she entered in the under-twenty division and compounded this precocious triumph by scoring a double victory in the National Horse Show at Madison Square Garden. Inevitably, her lifelong equestrian experience influenced the development of her singular personal style and permeated many aspects of her self-presentation. The formalized rituals of horseback riding and of the foxhunt in particular, with its finely nuanced dress codes and absolute respect for tradition, accorded perfectly with her sense of history. The precision of detail, self-discipline, and fastidious attention to clothing and accessories required by these activities would all inform her approach to state dressing as first lady of the United States.

To a letter received by her press office asking how she had achieved her unfalteringly erect deportment, Jacqueline Kennedy at first instructed Letitia Baldrige to respond that it was the result of long years of horseback riding. Although she later thought better of releasing this patrician response, it was nevertheless an accurate assessment. Jacqueline Kennedy's physical composure and carriage were an essential part of her public image, and they certainly enabled her to wear with aplomb the rigidly constructed clothes she favored for her official duties. As first lady, she remained passionate about horses and foxhunting, in spite of their inherent dangers (injuries she had sustained while riding included a broken collarbone and a slipped disc, and she was knocked unconscious during a hunt in Virginia in 1951). On her overseas tours equestrian divertissements were often built into her schedule. In Vienna, for instance, she took time to see the magisterial Lipizzaner horses at the Spanish Riding School, and in Jaipur she attended a polo match (the maharaja of Jaipur was a keen player). President Mohammad Ayub Khan of Pakistan, an enthusiastic rider himself, presented her with a magnificent bay gelding named Sardar.

Jacqueline Kennedy was also sensitive to picturesque effects. When snow fell on Washington in February 1962, for instance, she ordered a sleigh to be brought up from Glen Ora, the Kennedys' Virginia farm, along with Caroline's pony, Macaroni. She then took Caroline and some of her young friends for a sleigh ride across the White House lawns in a scene evocative of Currier and Ives. She could be just as sensitive, however, to the aristocratic implications of such a scene. In response to a journalist's query, Jacqueline Kennedy told her press secretary, Pamela Turnure, to "stress [that] I couldn't have my own pony until I was old enough to care for him—Believe children should do that. Had to rub her down . . . feed her . . . clean tack after each ride—And groom her." Nevertheless, in her riding clothes and accoutrements, as in the wardrobes she assembled for her children, Jacqueline Kennedy expressed traditional Anglophile tastes.

James Lock and Company (English, established 1676). Hunt cap ("Quorn") in black velvet. □ Riding derby in black wool felt. □ The form of the cap below (left) was derived from the eighteenth-century jockey cap, which was matched to the racing colors of the horse's owner. Black velvet examples were recorded in 1774, as part of a Quaker hunt uniform adopted by Philadelphia's Gloucester hunt. The shape evolved into its present "hard hat" to protect against head injuries in case of a fall. This one bears the label of Lock and Company, the preeminent London hatters, who had exported to America since 1781. In the American style it is worn "tails up," meaning that the tails of the grosgrain ribbon bow do not dip below the line of the hat. In Britain they hang down. This shape is named "Quorn," after the famous hunt in Leicestershire, England, and was created by Lock and Company. □ The nineteenth-century English hatmaker William Bowler invented his eponymous hat in 1850 for William Coke, who intended it for the gamekeepers on his Norfolk estate, Holkham Hall. Coke had requested a riding hat that would withstand rough treatment and fit close to the head so that it could not be easily dislodged. He tested Bowler's prototype by jumping on it. In America the form is also known as the derby, after the twelfth earl of Derby. As bowler, derby, or "extra-firm Coke," it has been a traditional alternative to a top hat or riding cap for hunting since the 1920s.

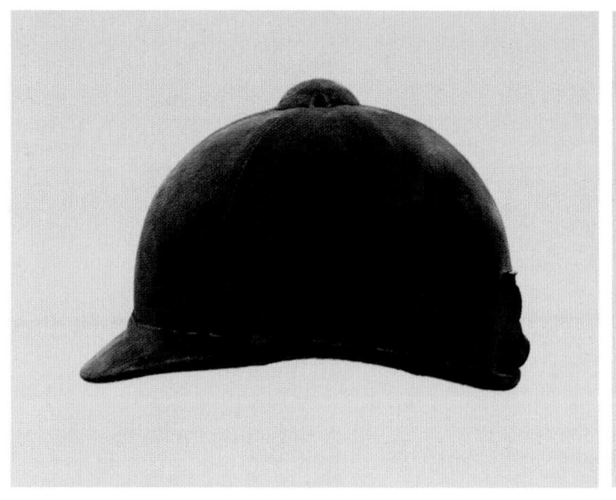

Riding coat in dun-and-wine wool plaid, ca. 1962. Riding with the President's Guard, New Delhi, March 14, 1962. Riding Sardar, Middleburg, Virginia, September 6, 1962. □ Riding coat in brown-and-green wool check, ca. 1961. Participating in a foxhunt, Upperville, Virginia, November 1961. □ The shape of the traditional riding coat shown above, with its almost sculptural tailoring defining the sleeves' curve and the long skirt's stiff flare, had been formalized since the 1920s. Jacqueline Kennedy's mother, Janet Lee Auchincloss, had similar examples in her own equestrian wardrobe, and it is probable that this one originally belonged to her. Mrs. Kennedy wore the coat when she accompanied ten officers of President Rajendra Prasad's guard on the polo grounds of his residence in New Delhi. Still dressed in riding clothes, she then watched a snake charmer in Prime Minister Jawaharlal Nehru's gardens, a divertissement that ended with a dramatic fight between a mongoose and a cobra. She also wore the coat in Middleburg, Virginia, during a private visit paid by Pakistan's president, Mohammad Ayub Khan. On this occasion Mrs. Kennedy rode Sardar (top right), the bay gelding that Ayub Khan had presented to her during her tour of his country. □ Jacqueline Kennedy wore the other riding coat shown here for a foxhunt on the Paul Mellons' Virginia estate. During the hunt her horse, Bit of Irish, balked at a split-rail fence and sent her flying. Photographer Marshall Hawkins was on hand to record the ignominy, but Mrs. Kennedy was game enough to consent to the publication of his photographs—and to have the resulting *Life* magazine spread included among the precious objects that were memorialized for her by Jansen's artist Pierre-Marie Rudelle in the trompe-l'oeil wardrobe doors of her White House dressing room.

Jacqueline Bouvier Kennedy: A Time Line, 1929–1994

1929
JULY 28 Jacqueline Lee Bouvier is born in Southampton, Long Island, New York, to Janet Lee and John Vernou Bouvier III. She spends her childhood in New York City and on Long Island.

1933
MARCH 3 Her sister, Caroline Lee Bouvier, is born.

1940
JULY 22 Janet and John Bouvier divorce.

1942
JUNE Janet Bouvier marries Hugh D. Auchincloss Jr. They reside in McLean, Virginia, and summer in Newport, Rhode Island.

1944
SEPTEMBER Jacqueline Bouvier enrolls at Miss Porter's School in Farmington, Connecticut. She joins the drama and riding clubs and is a cartoonist and editor for the student newspaper.

1947
SEPTEMBER Enrolls at Vassar College.

1949
AUGUST Begins her junior year in France, where she studies at the University of Grenoble and at the Sorbonne. In Paris she lives with the de Renty family.

1950
SEPTEMBER Transfers to George Washington University. She graduates the following May with a B. A. degree in French literature.

1951
MAY Wins *Vogue's* Prix de Paris writing contest. Her entry includes an essay describing three figures from history she wishes she had known: Charles Baudelaire, Oscar Wilde, and Serge Diaghilev.

MAY Introduced to Congressman John F. Kennedy of Massachusetts at a dinner party hosted by their mutual friends Charles and Martha Bartlett.

1952
JANUARY Begins working as the "Inquiring Camera Girl" for the Washington *Times Herald*. Among those she interviews for her daily column are John F. Kennedy and Richard M. Nixon. She covers the first inauguration of Dwight D. Eisenhower and the coronation of Queen Elizabeth II.

NOVEMBER 4 John F. Kennedy is elected to the United States Senate, defeating Republican incumbent Henry Cabot Lodge Jr.

1953
JUNE 23 Engagement of Jacqueline Bouvier to John F. Kennedy is announced.

SEPTEMBER 12 John F. Kennedy and Jacqueline Bouvier are married at Saint Mary's Church in Newport, Rhode Island. They honeymoon in Acapulco, Mexico.

1954
OCTOBER 21 John F. Kennedy undergoes serious back surgery for an injury suffered during World War II and endures more surgery the following February. During his convalescence he writes *Profiles in Courage* with encouragement from his wife, to whom the book is dedicated. Published in January 1956, it is awarded the 1957 Pulitzer Prize for biography.

1956
AUGUST 18 At the Democratic National Convention John F. Kennedy narrowly loses a bid for the vice-presidential nomination to Estes Kefauver.

1957
NOVEMBER 27 Caroline Bouvier Kennedy is born.

1958
NOVEMBER 4 John F. Kennedy is elected to a second term in the United States Senate.

1960
JANUARY 2 John F. Kennedy declares his presidential candidacy.

JANUARY 25 Jacqueline Kennedy joins her husband in New Hampshire to begin his campaign for the Democratic presidential nomination.

JULY 13 Senator Kennedy is nominated for president at the Democratic National Convention in Los Angeles. He chooses Senate Majority Leader Lyndon B. Johnson of Texas as his running mate.

SEPTEMBER 26 Senator Kennedy and the Republican nominee, Vice President Richard M. Nixon, appear in the first presidential debate to be broadcast live on television.

OCTOBER 19 Two million people cheer Senator and Mrs. Kennedy at a New York City ticker-tape parade. Then, in the late stages of her pregnancy, Jacqueline Kennedy curtails her campaign schedule and, from Hyannis Port, begins writing a weekly column entitled "Campaign Wife," which is published in newspapers around the country.

NOVEMBER 8 John F. Kennedy defeats Richard M. Nixon in the presidential election.

NOVEMBER 25 John F. Kennedy Jr. is born.

1961

JANUARY 20 John F. Kennedy is inaugurated as thirty-fifth president of the United States. He is the youngest elected president and the first Roman Catholic to hold the office. Jacqueline Kennedy becomes the third-youngest first lady.

JANUARY 25 John F. Kennedy conducts the first presidential press conference to be televised live.

FEBRUARY 23 The first lady announces the formation of the twelve-member Fine Arts Committee for the White House to develop restoration plans and acquire furnishings with ties to White House history. She names as chairman Henry Francis du Pont, a respected authority on American decorative art.

MARCH 1 President Kennedy signs an executive order establishing the Peace Corps.

MARCH 13 President Kennedy proposes the Alliance for Progress, an initiative on the part of the United States and the countries of Latin America emphasizing democratic reform and economic development.

MARCH 29 At the request of Mrs. Kennedy, Lorraine Pearce is appointed the first curator of the White House.

APRIL 12 Soviet cosmonaut Yuri Gagarin is the first person to orbit the earth.

APRIL 17 Fidel Castro's forces repel a U.S.-sponsored invasion of Cuba at the Bay of Pigs.

MAY 2 A 1778 drawing of Benjamin Franklin is the first major acquisition of the Fine Arts Committee for the White House.

MAY 3 At the first state dinner of the Kennedy administration the president and first lady honor President Habib Bourguiba of Tunisia.

MAY 5 Alan B. Shepard Jr. becomes the first American in space.

MAY 16 President and Mrs. Kennedy arrive in Ottawa, Canada, for their first state visit.

MAY 24 Prince Rainier and Princess Grace of Monaco visit the White House.

MAY 25 In a special address to Congress, President Kennedy urges a national commitment to land a man on the moon before 1970.

MAY 31 President and Mrs. Kennedy arrive in Paris for a three-day official visit, during which President Charles de Gaulle entertains them at Versailles.

JUNE 2 In response to Parisians' enthusiasm for his wife, President Kennedy introduces himself at a press conference as "the man who accompanied Jacqueline Kennedy to Paris."

JUNE 3 At a summit meeting in Vienna the Soviet premier, Nikita Khrushchev, warns President Kennedy belligerently that the western Allies must leave Berlin.

JUNE 4 The Kennedys arrive in London for the christening of their niece Anna Christina Radziwill. Later, they dine with Queen Elizabeth and Prince Philip at Buckingham Palace.

JULY 3 The Fine Arts Committee for the White House announces acquisitions of furniture belonging to Presidents Washington, Lincoln, Madison, Monroe, and Van Buren.

JULY 11 President Mohammad Ayub Khan of Pakistan is honored by the Kennedys at Mount Vernon in the first state dinner to be staged outside the White House.

JULY 25 President Kennedy activates the reserves and requests increases in military spending in response to tensions in Berlin.

AUGUST 12 Construction of the Berlin Wall begins.

AUGUST 22 The first Concert for Young People, sponsored by Mrs. Kennedy to encourage the study and performance of music by America's youth, is held on the South Lawn of the White House.

SEPTEMBER 21 Public Law 87–286, championed by Mrs. Kennedy, is approved by Congress, making the White House a national monument.

SEPTEMBER 22 The Interstate Commerce Commission approves Attorney General Robert Kennedy's petition to ban racial segregation in interstate bus travel.

NOVEMBER 3 The White House Historical Association is incorporated at Jacqueline Kennedy's behest. At the National Gallery of Art she opens the "Tutankhamun's Treasures" exhibition, then receives an ancient statue from Giza as a gift from President Gamal Abdel Nasser of Egypt, acknowledging the Kennedys' involvement in preserving the temples at Abu Simbel.

NOVEMBER 13 Spanish cellist Pablo Casals performs at the White House after a state dinner for Governor Luis Muñoz Marín of Puerto Rico.

NOVEMBER 25 The White House Paintings Committee is formed to acquire works of art for the White House collection.

DECEMBER 14 John F. Kennedy establishes the President's Commission on the Status of Women.

DECEMBER 15 President and Mrs. Kennedy embark on state visits to Puerto Rico, Venezuela, and Colombia.

1962

JANUARY 18 The refurbished Red Room of the White House, restored in the Empire style, is opened to the public.

FEBRUARY 14 Mrs. Kennedy hosts a televised tour of the White House, produced by CBS. The first lady later receives a special Emmy Award for public service from the National Academy of Television Arts and Sciences.

FEBRUARY 15 The Fine Arts Committee for the White House announces receipt of 240 objects of historic furniture and art and $134,000 in contributions.

FEBRUARY 20 Mezzo-soprano Grace Bumbry presents a recital in the East Room after a White House dinner for Vice President Lyndon Johnson, Speaker of the House John McCormack, and Chief Justice Earl Warren.

FEBRUARY 20 Astronaut John H. Glenn Jr. becomes the first American to orbit the earth.

MARCH 11 En route to a semiofficial two-week visit to India and Pakistan, Mrs. Kennedy stops in Rome for a private audience with Pope John XXIII.

MARCH 12 In New Delhi, Prime Minister Jawaharlal Nehru of India welcomes the first lady and her sister, Princess Radziwill.

MARCH 21 Mrs. Kennedy and Princess Radziwill arrive in Lahore, Pakistan. President Mohammad Ayub Khan presents the first lady with a bay gelding, Sardar, at the Lahore Horse Show.

MARCH 26 Mrs. Kennedy makes a three-day stop in London, where she has lunch with Queen Elizabeth II.

APRIL 29 President and Mrs. Kennedy welcome forty-nine Nobel prizewinners from the Western Hemisphere to a White House dinner held in their honor.

MAY 8 Jacqueline Kennedy launches the Polaris submarine USS *Lafayette*.

MAY 11 André Malraux, the minister of cultural affairs for the Republic of France, is honored at a White House dinner.

JUNE 21 The refurbished White House Library opens.

JUNE 24 The White House Rose Garden, redesigned by Rachel Lambert Mellon, is completed.

JUNE 28 President and Mrs. Kennedy receive copies of *The White House: An Historic Guide*, the first publication of the White House Historical Association. The restored Treaty Room opens with facsimiles of treaties signed in the late nineteenth century, when it served as the Cabinet Room.

JUNE 29 President and Mrs. Kennedy arrive in Mexico for a two-day official visit.

SEPTEMBER 11 In Newport, Rhode Island, the first lady unveils architect Edward Durell Stone's model for the proposed National Cultural Center to be built in Washington, D.C.

SEPTEMBER 26 Jacqueline Kennedy inspects revised plans for Washington's Lafayette Square across from the White House. After discovering that the square's eighteenth-century townhouses were to be demolished for a government office building, Mrs. Kennedy had led a successful last-minute effort to save them. The new plans incorporate the historic structures into the design.

SEPTEMBER 28 President Kennedy orders the U.S. military to enforce a court order to enroll James Meredith as the first African-American student at the University of Mississippi.

OCTOBER 16 President Kennedy is shown aerial photographs of Soviet nuclear missile bases in Cuba. The weapons threaten most major American cities. Facing the threat of nuclear war, President Kennedy orders a U.S. blockade of the island. After almost two weeks of tense negotiations, Premier Khrushchev orders the dismantling of the bases on October 28.

NOVEMBER 15 The Kennedys host a private White House tour for Moscow's Bolshoi Ballet.

NOVEMBER 30 A thirty-minute film of the first lady's visit to India and Pakistan, *Jacqueline Kennedy's Asian Journey*, is released to movie theaters worldwide.

DECEMBER 29 At the Orange Bowl in Miami President and Mrs. Kennedy address members of Brigade 2506, which participated in the failed Bay of Pigs invasion of Cuba.

1963

JANUARY 8 The Mona Lisa is exhibited at the National Gallery of Art in Washington D.C. France had permitted the shipment of the painting to the United States as a personal loan to President Kennedy.

JANUARY 21 The Blue Room, reflecting President Monroe's taste for French furnishings, and the Green Room, decorated in American Federal style, both open to the public.

MARCH 18 President Kennedy meets with Central American presidents in Costa Rica to discuss economic and security issues.

APRIL 15 Mrs. Kennedy cancels all of her official engagements until after the birth of her third child.

MAY 11 President Kennedy tours the Boston area to inspect possible sites for his presidential library.

MAY 17 Sales of *The White House: An Historic Guide* reach half a million copies.

JUNE 10 At American University, President Kennedy proposes a "strategy of peace" to lead the U.S. and U.S.S.R. out of the nuclear arms race. He also signs the Equal Pay Act, requiring that women receive equal pay for equal work.

JUNE 11 President Kennedy mobilizes the National Guard to enforce admission of black students to the University of Alabama.

JUNE 24 President Kennedy visits the Berlin Wall and receives a hero's welcome when he addresses a huge crowd afterward: "Ich bin ein Berliner."

AUGUST 7 Patrick Bouvier Kennedy is born prematurely. Suffering from respiratory distress, he dies two days later.

AUGUST 28 Dr. Martin Luther King Jr. delivers his "I Have a Dream" speech at the Lincoln Memorial. President Kennedy meets with Dr. King and other organizers of the March on Washington in the Oval Office.

AUGUST 30 The "hot line" between the Kremlin and the White House is established.

OCTOBER 10 President Kennedy signs the Limited Nuclear Test Ban Treaty in the Treaty Room. The treaty, which had been negotiated by the United States, the Soviet Union, and the United Kingdom, prohibits the testing of nuclear weapons in the atmosphere and in the oceans.

OCTOBER 26 President Kennedy speaks at Amherst College in Massachusetts: "I look forward to an America that will not be afraid of grace and beauty . . . that will reward achievement in the arts as well as achievement in business or statecraft."

NOVEMBER 1 The first of more than two million Christmas cards designed by the first lady are sold to benefit the National Cultural Center.

NOVEMBER 13 President and Mrs. Kennedy join 1,700 Washington-area children on the White House South Lawn for a performance by the Pipes and Drums of the Black Watch, a Scottish regiment of the British Army.

NOVEMBER 21 President and Mrs. Kennedy depart the White House for a three-day tour of Texas.

NOVEMBER 22 President Kennedy is assassinated in Dallas.

NOVEMBER 25 John F. Kennedy is buried at Arlington National Cemetery. Jacqueline Kennedy lights the eternal flame.

1964

SEPTEMBER Jacqueline Kennedy and her children move to New York City.

NOVEMBER 3 Robert F. Kennedy is elected to the United States Senate, representing New York.

1968

MARCH 15 Senator Robert F. Kennedy announces his candidacy for the presidency of the United States.

JUNE 6 Robert F. Kennedy is assassinated in Los Angeles. Two days later he is buried at Arlington National Cemetery.

OCTOBER 20 Jacqueline Kennedy marries Greek shipping magnate Aristotle Onassis on the island of Skorpios.

1975

JANUARY Jacqueline Kennedy Onassis becomes involved in the fight to save New York City's Grand Central Station from demolition.

MARCH 15 Aristotle Onassis dies in Paris.

1976

SEPTEMBER 22 Jacqueline Kennedy Onassis begins her career in publishing by joining the staff of the Viking Press as a literary editor. In 1978 she moves to Doubleday and Company, where she edits, among other books, *Allure*, by Diana Vreeland; *The Cairo Trilogy*, by Naguib Mahfouz; *Learning to Look: My Life in Art*, by John Pope-Hennessy; and *Louis XIV: A Royal Life*, by Olivier Bernier.

1979

OCTOBER 20 Jacqueline Kennedy Onassis joins the Kennedy family, President Jimmy Carter, and 10,000 spectators in Boston at the dedication of the John F. Kennedy Library and Museum designed by I. M. Pei.

1994

MAY 19 Jacqueline Bouvier Kennedy Onassis dies in New York City. Four days later she is buried at Arlington National Cemetery.

Notes on Sources

Publishing data is provided for works not listed in the Bibliography.

"Jacqueline Kennedy in the White House"

Jacqueline Kennedy's papers are in the John F. Kennedy Library, Boston. I have also drawn on several memoirs: Letitia Baldrige, *Of Diamonds and Diplomats*; Clark M. Clifford with Richard Holbrooke, *Counsel to the President: A Memoir* (New York: Random House, 1991); Richard N. Goodwin, *Remembering America* (Boston: Little, Brown, 1988); Pierre Salinger, *With Kennedy* (Garden City, New York: Doubleday and Company, 1966); J. B. West with Mary Lynn Kotz, *Upstairs at the White House: My Life with the First Ladies*. Among secondary works, these were especially useful: Carl Sferrazza Anthony, *As We Remember Her*; Carl Sferrazza Anthony, *First Ladies: The Saga of the Presidents' Wives and Their Power. Volume II: 1961–1990*; Apple Parish Bartlett and Susan Bartlett Crater, *Sister: The Life of Legendary American Interior Decorator, Mrs. Henry Parish II*; Sarah Bradford, *America's Queen: The Life of Jacqueline Kennedy Onassis*; Norman Mailer, *The Presidential Papers* (New York: G. P. Putnam's Sons, 1963); Arthur M. Schlesinger Jr., *A Thousand Days: John F. Kennedy in the White House* (Boston: Houghton Mifflin, 1965); Mary Van Rensselaer Thayer, *Jacqueline Kennedy: The White House Years*. AMSJR.

"Defining Style: Jacqueline Kennedy's White House Years"

The archives of the John F. Kennedy Library and Museum proved invaluable in the preparation of this catalogue, and of my introductory essay in particular. I have also drawn upon interviews conducted with Alexandre de Paris, Kenneth Battelle, Joseph Boccheir, Marc Bohan, Donald Brooks, Bob Bugnand, Oleg Cassini, Eleanor Dwight, Hubert de Givenchy, C. Z. Guest, Leopold Kobrin, Eleanor Lambert, Mary McFadden, Kay McGowan, Rachel Lambert Mellon, Lee Radziwill, D. D. Ryan, Babs Simpson, Annette Tapert, Gustave Tassell, and Jayne Wrightsman. In addition, I wish to acknowledge unpublished material by James A. Abbott on the White House restoration.

The library of the Costume Institute at the Metropolitan Museum, the archives of Condé Nast Publications, and the archives of Fairchild Publications were major sources for journals and periodicals from the Kennedy White House years, from which I have quoted extensively. I have also drawn particularly upon the following publications: Carl Sferrazza Anthony, *First Ladies: The Saga of the Presidents' Wives and Their Power. Volume I, 1789–1961; Volume II, 1961–1990*; Bettina Ballard, *In My Fashion*; Cecil Beaton, *The Restless Years: Diaries, 1955–63*; Marilyn Bender, *The Beautiful People* (New York: Coward-McCann, 1967); Jacqueline Bouvier and Lee Bouvier, *One Special Summer* (New York: Delacorte Press, 1974); Sarah Bradford, *America's Queen: The Life of Jacqueline Kennedy Onassis*; James Brady, *Superchic*; Pearl S. Buck, *The Kennedy Women: A Personal Appraisal*; Oleg Cassini, *A Thousand Days of Magic: Dressing Jacqueline Kennedy for the White House* (New York: Rizzoli, 1995); Oleg Cassini, *In My Own Fashion: An Autobiography* (New York: Simon and Schuster, 1987); Rose Fitzgerald Kennedy, *Times to Remember*; Phyllis Lee Levin, *The Wheels of Fashion*; Betty C. Monkman, *The White House: Its Historic Furnishings & First Families* (Washington D.C.: White House Historical Association; New York: Abbeville Press, 2000); Mini Rhea, *I Was Jacqueline Kennedy's Dressmaker*; Robert Riley and Walter Vecchio, *The Fashion Makers: A Photographic Record*; Bernard Roshco, *The Rag Race* (New York: Funk and Wagnalls Company, 1963); Mary Van Rensselaer Thayer, *Jacqueline Kennedy: The White House Years*; Diana Vreeland, *D.V.* HB

Bibliography

Aarons, Slim. *A Wonderful Time: An Intimate Portrait of the Good Life.* New York: Harper and Row, 1975.

Abbott, James A. *A Frenchman in Camelot: The Decoration of the Kennedy White House by Stéphane Boudin*. Garrison-on-Hudson, New York: Boscobel Restoration, 1995.

Abbott, James A., and Elaine M. Rice. *Designing Camelot: The Kennedy White House Restoration*. New York: Van Nostrand Reinhold, 1998.

Anthony, Carl Sferrazza. *As We Remember Her.* Harper Collins Publishers, 1997.

———. *First Ladies: The Saga of the Presidents' Wives and Their Power. Volume I: 1789–1961*. New York: William Morrow and Company, 1990; *Volume II: 1961–1990*. New York: William Morrow and Company, 1991.

Baldrige, Letitia. *In the Kennedy Style: Magical Evenings in the Kennedy White House*. Garden City, New York: Doubleday, 1998.

———. *Of Diamonds and Diplomats*. Boston: Houghton Mifflin Company, 1968.

Baldwin, Billy. *Billy Baldwin Remembers*. New York: Harcourt Brace Jovanovich, 1974.

Ballard, Bettina. *In My Fashion*. New York: David McKay Company, 1960.

Bartlett, Apple Parish, and Susan Bartlett Crater. *Sister: The Life of Legendary American Interior Decorator, Mrs. Henry Parish II*. New York: St. Martin's Press, 2000.

Beaton, Cecil. *The Restless Years: Diaries, 1955–63*. London: Weidenfeld and Nicolson, 1976.

Bergquist, Laura, and Stanley Tretick. *A Very Special President*. New York: McGraw Hill, 1965.

Bradford, Sarah. *America's Queen: The Life of Jacqueline Kennedy Onassis*. New York: Viking, 2000.

Brady, James. *Superchic*. Boston: Little, Brown and Company, 1974.

Buck, Pearl S. *The Kennedy Women: A Personal Appraisal*. New York: Cowles Book Company, 1970.

Davis, John H. *The Bouviers: Portrait of an American Family*. New York: Farrar, Straus and Giroux, 1969.

———. *Jacqueline Bouvier: An Intimate Memoir*. New York: John Wiley and Sons, 1996.

Duhême, Jacqueline. *Mrs. Kennedy Goes Abroad*. New York: Artisan, 1998.

Faber, Harold, and Jacques Lowe. *The Kennedy Years*. New York: Viking Press, 1964.

Fairchild, John. *The Fashionable Savages*. Garden City, New York: Doubleday and Company, 1965.

Gaines, Steven S. *Simply Halston: The Untold Story*. New York: G. P. Putnam's Sons, 1991.

Gallagher, Mary Barelli. *My Life with Jacqueline Kennedy*. New York: David McKay Company, 1969.

Gross, Elaine, and Fred Rottman. *Halston: An American Original*. New York: Harper Collins, 1999.

Hellman, Joan Rattner, ed. *Kenneth's Complete Book on Hair*. New York: Doubleday, 1969.

Kennedy, Rose Fitzgerald. *Times to Remember*. New York: Doubleday, 1995.

Koestenbaum, Wayne. *Jackie under My Skin: Interpreting an Icon*. New York: Farrar, Straus and Giroux, 1995.

Leish, Kenneth W. *The White House*. New York: Newsweek, 1972.

Levin, Phyllis Lee. *The Wheels of Fashion*. Garden City, New York: Doubleday and Company, 1965.

Lincoln, Anne H. *The Kennedy White House Parties*. New York: Viking Press, 1967.

Lincoln, Evelyn. *My Twelve Years with John F. Kennedy*. New York: David McKay Company, 1965.

Lowe, Jacques. *JFK Remembered*. New York: Random House, 1993.

———. *Portrait: The Emergence of John F. Kennedy*. New York: Bramhall House, 1961.

Rhea, Mini. *I Was Jacqueline Kennedy's Dressmaker*. New York: Fleet Publishing, 1962.

Riley, Robert, and Walter Vecchio. *The Fashion Makers: A Photographic Record*. Crown Publishers, 1968.

Sotheby's. *The Estate of Jacqueline Kennedy Onassis*. Sale cat., New York: Sotheby's, April 23–26, 1996.

———. *Property from the Collection of the Late Sister Parish*. Sale cat., New York: Sotheby's, September 29, 1995.

Sparks, Fred. *The $20,000,000 Honeymoon: Jackie and Ari's First Year*. New York: B. Geis Associates, 1970.

Tapert, Annette, and Diana Edkins. *The Power of Style: The Women Who Defined the Art of Living Well*. New York: Crown Publishers, 1994.

Thayer, Mary Van Rensselaer. *Jacqueline Kennedy: The White House Years*. Boston: Little, Brown and Company, 1971.

Verdon, René. *The White House Chef Cookbook*. Garden City, New York: Doubleday and Company, 1967.

Vreeland, Diana. *D.V.* New York: Alfred A. Knopf, 1984.

Walker, John. *Self-Portrait with Donors: Confessions of an Art Collector*. Boston: Little, Brown and Company, 1974.

West, J. B., with Mary Lynn Kotz. *Upstairs at the White House: My Life with the First Ladies*. New York: Coward, McCann and Geoghegan, 1973.

Wolff, Perry. *A Tour of the White House with Mrs. John F. Kennedy*. Garden City, New York: Doubleday and Company, 1962.

Acknowledgments

This publication and exhibition would not be possible without the gracious collaboration of Caroline Kennedy, who provided invaluable assistance in the preparation of the manuscript and throughout all stages of the exhibition design. In addition, I thank the staff of the John F. Kennedy Library and Museum for granting the authors permission to use their archives and for crucial help with many components of the catalogue and exhibition. I am particularly indebted to Maria Carosa Stanwich, Frank Rigg, Megan Floyd Desnoyers, Allan Goodrich, and Elizabeth Stapleton-Roach for their enthusiasm and tireless efforts. Sarah Hast, James Hill, April Kierstead, Tom McNaught, Tom Putnam, Kristine Rhoback, Sam Rubin, Lee Statham, Victoria Tise, and Pamela Winstead also provided important help and support. Many thanks to James Wagner for his excellent research and extraordinary commitment to this project, as well as to Edwin A. Schlossberg and Amy Forman.

I greatly appreciate the work of many staff members of The Metropolitan Museum of Art. At the Costume Institute, special thanks are due to Harold Koda, for his stimulating insights and knowledge; as well as to Myra Walker and Christine Paulocik. Carmela Tigani, Maya Nauton, Alexandra Kowalski, Melinda Webber, Jennifer Cole, and Michael Downer worked tirelessly to construct and prepare the mannequins photographed for this catalogue, which were dressed with skill and nuance by Lisa Faibish and meticulously photographed by Karin L. Willis. Monique van Dorp, Tara McNeill, Amy Beil, and Shannon Bell handled the myriad administrative details of this project with efficiency and grace. Michelle Tolini, Karine Prot, Hanna Nordgren, Jenni McSpadden, Natalia Rand, and Stéphane Houy-Towner provided thorough and enthusiastic research assistance. In addition to the staff of the Costume Institute, Emily Rafferty, Doralynn Pines, Linda Sylling, and Nina Maruca supported this project with gracious and much appreciated forbearance. I applaud the entire exhibition design team for their inspired work, especially Jeff Daly, Dennis Kois, Zack Zanolli, Christopher Noey, and Sophia Geronimus.

Sam Shahid of Shahid and Company complemented the elegant subject of this exhibition with his deft catalogue design. His associates Betty Eng and Frederico Farina displayed patience and good humor in the face of intense deadlines. Charles D. Scheips Jr. and Stephanie Ovide Guarneri worked exhaustively on picture research, and we acknowledge the great support of Susan Train, Paris bureau chief of American *Vogue*, during the making of this publication. I thank Jane Stubbs for her independent research on this project and Annette Tapert for generously sharing her own research materials with me. Thanks are also due to the following people from various photograph agencies and archives and to the photographers who contributed to this catalogue: Jennifer Bikel, Fairchild Publications; Anne Bouteloup, Éditions Gallimard; Ron Brenne and Elysa Sachar, UPI/Corbis-Bettmann; Woody Camp, Woodfin Camp and Associates; Chapin Carson, Sotheby's; Maureen Catbagan, the Metropolitan Museum; Cynthia Cathcart, Michael Stier, Thomas Graf, and Ena Wojciechowski, Condé Nast Publications; Juliet Cuming and Susan Goldstein, Mark Shaw Photographic Archive; Rosa Di Salvo, Liaison Agency; David Fahey, Fahey/Klein Gallery;

Anne Garsile, Peabody Institute of the Johns Hopkins University; Tom Gilberg and Jennifer McAlwee, Time Pix; Yvette Gordon, AP World Wide; Beno Grazziani; Claudine Legros, *Paris Match*; Cathy Levelle, Archive Photos; Jacques Lowe; David Lombard, CBS; Fred J. Maroon; Anthony Mazzola and Steve Rogers, *Harper's Bazaar*; Alex Moore and Vanessa Noll-Mack, Corbis Sygma; Natasha O'Connor, Magnum Photos; Justin O'Neill, FPG International; Patti Vento, Parade Publications; William Phillips and Harmony Haskins, White House Historical Association; Jerome Rankine, *Newsweek*; Josh Schmidt and Norma Stevens, Avedon Studio; Kathy Struff, Dwight D. Eisenhower Library; Marie-Jose Susskind, *L'Officiel*; Joshua Walden, Fashion Institute of Technology Library.

In addition to the above, I am deeply grateful to the following individuals and institutions for their valued assistance: James A. Abbott; Adolfo Sardiña; Alexandre de Paris; Mrs. Douglas Auchincloss; Kenneth Battelle; Geoffrey Beene; Mrs. William McCormick Blair Jr.; Kenneth Paul Block; Steven Bluttal; Joseph Mark Boccheir; Marc Bohan; Donald Brooks; Bob Bugnand; John Carlin and Steven D. Tilley, National Archives and Records Administration; Pierre Cardin; Oleg Cassini; La Maison Chanel; Lan du Chastel and Marc Stoltz, Hermès; Crespi and Mariani Associates; Devie Deland, *Vogue*; Tiffany Dubin; Jacqueline Duhême; Eleanor Dwight; George Dwight; Tom Fallon; Amy Fine Collins; Federico Forquet; Odile Fraigneau, Lanvin Archives; Bill Frappier, Goldsmith Mannequins; Steven Gaines; James Galanos; Giancarlo Giammetti; Hubert de Givenchy; Mrs. Winston F. C. Guest; Albert Hadley; Gale Hayman; Jean-Pascal Hesse, Pierre Cardin; Hugh Holland and Laura Mingay, Wetherill; Marie-Andrée Jouve, Balenciaga Archives; Peter Kent; Pamela Keogh; Michelle Kessler, *Vogue*; Leopold Kobrin; Peter Krauss, Ursus Books; Bernice Kwok-Gabel, the Metropolitan Museum; Mylène Lajoix, Givenchy Couture Archives; Eleanor Lambert; Ralph Lauren; Mary McFadden; Kay McGowan; Mrs. Paul Mellon; Caroline Rennolds Milbank; Richard Nelson; Serene O'Connor; Joelle Palazon, Nina Ricci Archives; Soizic Pffaf, Christian Dior Couture Archives; Jean-Philippe Pons, Yves Saint Laurent Archives; Roger Prigent; Laudomia Pucci; Lee Radziwill; Iann Roland-Bourgade, Paris bureau, American *Vogue*; Pierre-Marie Rudelle; D. D. Ryan; Kumiko Sakurai, Atelier Hinode; Sidney Schroeger; Audrey Schilts; Sandy Schreier; Rose Simon; Babs Simpson; Daniel Storto; Gustave Tassell; Janet Taylor, James Lock and Co.; D. D. Tillett; Nancy Tuckerman; Frederick Vreeland; Thomas R. Vreeland; Lillian Wang von Stauffenberg, Verdura; Charles Whitehouse; Deidre Windsor and the staff of the Textile Conservation Center, Lowell, Massachusetts; Mrs. Charles Wrightsman.

I am indebted to Anna Wintour for her tremendous support during this project and for her professional generosity in allowing me the time to work on it. I owe another great debt to Philippe de Montebello for putting his faith in my involvement in this project and for giving both the exhibition and the catalogue his attentive backing. Finally, my heartfelt thanks to the editorial team at the Metropolitan Museum, especially John P. O'Neill, Joan Holt, Peter Antony, and Jennifer Bernstein for their wry humor and fortitude.

Photograph Credits

New color photography of garments and accessories by Karin L. Willis of the Photograph Studio, The Metropolitan Museum of Art. All other photographs provided by the John F. Kennedy Library and Museum unless otherwise noted below.

© HOWARD O. ALLEN, 186 © ARCHIVE PHOTOS, 187 (bottom) © ABBIE ROWE, NATIONAL ARCHIVES, 18 (center right) AP/WIDE WORLD PHOTOS, 19 (bottom), 32 (bottom), 63, 75 (bottom), 152, 157, 170, 184 (Courtesy of the John F. Kennedy Library), 188 (bottom left), 189 (top right) © RICHARD AVEDON, cover (January 3, 1961); 79 (January 3, 1961) RENÉ BOUCHÉ, PROPERTY OF ROGER PRIGENT, 29 (bottom) © 2000 CBS WORLDWIDE, INC., 71 © CORBIS SYGMA, 54 © CORNELL CAPA/MAGNUM PHOTOS, INC., 52 (bottom), 130–31 THE DIOR ARCHIVES, 32 (top left), 32 (top center; Eduardo Latour), 33 (top left) COURTESY OF *EBONY* MAGAZINE © 1962 JOHNSON PUBLISHING COMPANY, 100 (top left) COURTESY OF THE FASHION INSTITUTE OF TECHNOLOGY LIBRARY, 124 (top center), 180 (top and bottom) © JACQUELINE DUHÊME, COURTESY OF THE JOHN F. KENNEDY LIBRARY, 124 (bottom), 153 (top right) © FPG INTERNATIONAL LLC, 129 (top left) © *HOUSE AND GARDEN*, CONDÉ NAST PUBLICATIONS, 22 (bottom; Christian Reinhardt), 26 (bottom left and right; Tom Leonard) *LOOK* MAGAZINE, COURTESY OF THE LIBRARY OF CONGRESS, 34 (top left) © JACQUES LOWE, 36, 38, 39, 43, 47 (top left and right), 48 (bottom), 50, 57, 58, 60 (top), 62, 66 (bottom), 67, 75 (top), 118 (top right), 132, 189 (top left) THE GIVENCHY ARCHIVE, 21 (bottom right, clockwise), 22 (center left), 31 (bottom right), 33 (top center) © BENO GRAZZIANI, 175, 187 (top) © HULTON GETTY/LIAISON AGENCY, 18 (bottom left) © YOUSUF KARSH/WOODFIN CAMP AND ASSOCIATES, 21 (top) COURTESY OF CAROLINE KENNEDY, 20 (top) © FRED J. MAROON, 68 *L'OFFICIEL DE LA COUTURE ET DE LA MODE*, 31 (bottom left and center; Pottier), 109 (bottom) © *PARIS MATCH*, 118 (bottom; Habans), 121 (left; Le Tellier), 122 (top; Habans), 122 (center; Lagache), 123 (Courrière), 129 (top right), 140 (top; Beno Grazziani) © *QUEEN* MAGAZINE, THE NATIONAL MAGAZINE CO. LTD, 174 (top) RUE DES ARCHIVES, 118 (top left), 124 (top right) © STEVE SCHAPIRO, COURTESY FAHEY/KLEIN GALLERY, 182 © MARK SHAW/PHOTO RESEARCHERS, ii, 21 (bottom left), 40, 41, 44 (top left and right), 88 (top), 90–91, 176–77 © TIME PIX, 18 (top; Yale Joel/Courtesy of Sandy Schreier), 24 (bottom right; Ed Clark), 30 (top; Ralph Crane/Black Star), 60 (bottom; George Silk), 94 (bottom; Art Rickerby), 108 (bottom left; Art Rickerby), 117 (top right; Leonard McCombe/Courtesy of the John F. Kennedy Library) © UPI/CORBIS-BETTMANN, 22 (top; New York *Daily Mirror* Collection), 29 (top left), 44 (bottom), 48 (top), 53, 64, 106 (left), 109 (top), 113 (right), 122 (bottom), 135, 136 (top), 145, 150, 162 (top left), 192–93 © *VOGUE*, CONDÉ NAST PUBLICATIONS, 12 (Horst P. Horst), 15 (Horst P. Horst), 16 (René Bouché), 18 (center left; Ernst Beadle); 20 (bottom; Richard Rutledge), 25 (top; Henri Cartier-Bresson), 25 (bottom; Cecil Beaton), 29 (top right; Henry Koehler), 33 (bottom; Henry Clarke), 66 (top) © *WOMEN'S WEAR DAILY*, FAIRCHILD PUBLICATIONS, INC., 93 (top; November 19, 1961) THE WHITE HOUSE COLLECTION © WHITE HOUSE HISTORICAL ASSOCIATION, 24 (top)

Unless otherwise noted, the clothing and accessories are in the collections of the John F. Kennedy Library and Museum or are retained by the Kennedy family.